Awe God

Awe God

Seeing God in the Everyday Moments

Denise E. Johnson

Awe God

Copyright © 2024 Denise E. Johnson

All rights reserved. No portion of this book may be reproduced, stored in a retrieval system, or transmitted in any form or by any means; electronic, mechanical, photocopy, recording, scanning, or other without written permission from the publisher.

We extend our deepest gratitude to the countless scholars, translators, and scribes who have dedicated their lives to preserving and translating the sacred texts contained within the various version of the Bible. Their unwavering commitment to accurately transmitting the message of faith and wisdom has enriched the lives of countless individuals throughout history. We acknowledge the immense effort and dedication required to compile, translate, and disseminate these invaluable Scriptures, which serve as a beacon of guidance and inspiration to millions around the world.

Scripture quotations marked (MSG) are taken from *The Message,* copyright © 1993, 2002, 2018 by Eugene H. Peterson. Used by permission of NavPress. All rights reserved. Represented by Tyndale House Publishers. Scripture quotations marked (KJV) from The Authorized King James Version. Rights in the Authorized Version in the United Kingdom are vested in the Crown. Reproduced by permission of the Crown's patentee, Cambridge University Press. Scripture quotations marked (NIV) are taken from the Holy Bible, New International Version, copyright © 1973, 1978, 1984, 2011 by Biblica Inc. Used by permission of Zondervan. All rights reserved worldwide. Scripture quotations marked (ESV) are taken from English Standard Version Bible copyright © 2001 by Crossway, a publishing ministry of Good New Publishers. Used by permission. All rights reserved. References used: openbible.com and biblegateway.com

Book cover designed by Morgan Howell

Edited by Ron Johnson, Colleen Howell, Pamela Strong, and Suzie Kleppelid

ISBN 978-0-9984510-3-9

Start with Gratitude

Most major projects cannot happen without others coming alongside. Such is the case with Awe God. There is a certain irony to this book that God prompted me to write. One of my greatest challenges in my writing journey has been coming up with good titles. Then God put in my hands this book that required 100 titles! God has a way of giving us a work-out when there are areas we need to improve! I'm not sure that, left to my own accord, I would stretch and to grow so, thank you to my loving Father.

Next order of business is my profound thanks to the many people who, by choice or by force, became a subject of these writings. Some of you know who you are, some of you will be surprised to see your name on these pages, and some of you are simply anonymous. Thank you for being a part of revealing God's glory.

To my dear and treasured husband Ron: I'm not sure if I should say thank you or I'm sorry for allowing me to share the intimate and personal moments of our journey in life. As I wandered through these memories, I repeatedly felt immense gratitude that God gave me such a faithful and life-long partner (forty years and counting). The pages reflect a small slice of our life's adventures and through it all, I'm so grateful we hung in there together. Thank you for your attention to detail as you edited and critiqued each piece, often picking up on something I'd missed. You are my safe place, where I can be raw and vulnerable as we've matured from our starry-eyed days of courtship. Ron, you are the love of my life, now and forever.

To my sister Colleen: She's been my best friend since she entered my life at seventeen months old. Since then, we've shared clothes, friends, a bedroom, a bathroom, a car, our brother, secrets, tears, and many, many memories. A special thank you for always being my cheerleader, encourager, and accountability partner in life. Colleen really deserves the credit for my writing journey. She encouraged me to write my first book, **Love To Give**, which provided tremendous healing. Then she threw out the preposterous idea of writing a fictional book and sent me to a Christian Writers Conference. She covered all the expenses so I could rub shoulders with other authors, editors, and publishers. That resulted in my second book, **For The Children**. She set up my website, provided the brains on technology issues, and offered suggestions, being generous with compliments to keep me moving forward. Without Colleen, I might not have discovered the joy of sharing God's stories. Thank you, Sis. You've kept me sane and inspired me in ways I can't put into words. Can you believe it? I actually ran out of words!

I also owe a deep gratitude to the many who have read my stories, followed me on my website **DeniseEJohnson.com**, and encouraged me to keep writing. With a full and busy life, writing was sporadic at best. You expressed appreciation and helped me validate that God had given me this gift to write, one that fills my heart and gives me a sense of being centered, even when life is challenging.

Most importantly, I thank my gracious God who gave me this love of writing and brought Scripture to life in my daily experiences. He taught me that He can use an imperfect person to write an imperfect book to share His perfect story. Awe God. You are so good!

I hope you are blessed with these short stories of God's glory!

"Because we know that this extraordinary day is just ahead, we pray for you all the time—pray that our God will make you fit for what he's called you to be, pray that he'll fill your good ideas and acts of faith with his own energy so that it all amounts to something. If your life honors the name of Jesus, he will honor you. Grace is behind and through all of this, our God giving himself freely, the Master, Jesus Christ, giving himself freely." 2 Thessalonians 1:11-12 (MSG)

TABLE of CONTENTS

Fan the Flame 1
Dad's Final Question 3
Impossible Meeting 6
Mom's Comfort 8
Humph 10
Nick of Time 12
Go After Them 14
He Provides 16
Moving 19
The Strike 21
A Chinese Bible 23
Waiting for Baily 25
A Part-time Job 27
Be a Container 29
Seven Long Years 31
Perseverance 33
The Perfect Job 35
Wanted: Wisdom 37
What Divides Us 39
Help Wanted 41
To Africa 43
The Orphans 45
Back to Africa 47
Letting Go 49

Happy Birthday Amy	51
Africa Bound Again?	53
Seating Assignment	55
Something's Missing	57
Making Room	59
Time Out	61
Unexpected Flight	63
Going to Jail	65
Life's a Mess	67
New Hope	69
What a Bag!	71
Thy Will Be Done	73
The Quilt	75
Christmas Blessings	77
A New Thing	79
To-Do List	81
Stretch Marks	83
Misunderstood	85
Motherhood	87
Sweet and Sour	89
Falling Together	91
Time Well Spent	93
Behind the Scenes	95
The Labyrinth	97
I Can Only Imagine	99
Traditions	101

The Connection	103
Be Still	105
Downsizing	107
The Gift of Time	109
Laboring	111
Leave the Door Open	113
The Loan	115
Ripping Away	118
Day at the Beach	120
And That's the Truth	122
Genealogy – YAWN!	124
Suddenly Moments	126
Did You Get the Message?	128
Muddy Boots	130
Don't Forget Me	132
Heavenly Messages	134
Building a Family	136
The Bridge	140
Rocky Trails	142
By My Spirit	144
Her Hands	146
The Remnant	148
The Shepherd	150
What Lingers	152
The Comforter	154
Mom's Christmas Gift	156

The Wrong Porch	158
He Wins	160
Just Another Stat	163
So?	165
The Shorter Road	167
Listen Up	169
The Most Wonderful Time of the Year?	171
The Fun One	173
Surrounded	176
Traction	178
The Question	180
Tender Mercies	182
My Vacation	184
Running Out of Air	186
My Own Personal Snowstorm	188
Rebuilding	190
Random Reminders	192
Broken	194
She Chose Life	196
For Heaven's Sake	198
Just Ask	200
Oops!	202
Simple Treasurers	204
The Tapestry	206

Fan the Flame

Exhausted after claiming a few shredded hours of sleep, I dropped into my seat on the airplane and briefly greeted my seatmate. I settled in and before long, I conked out. The clanking of the service cart awakened me. The flight attendant asked if I'd like something to drink. Groggily I ordered a 7up to calm my stomach and then glanced at my seatmate. I realized she looked familiar. It took me a moment but then her name popped into my mind.

"Is your name Ginny?"

"Yes!" Her eyes widened as she looked at me.

"I think we went to college together."

Sure enough. Ginny and I had lived on the same floor our freshman year and had been in a service group our sophomore year. Time had changed her a bit, but not much. I should have recognized her. With our new realization, the conversation quickly changed to personal interests as we caught up on the past thirty plus years. How quickly our plane ride went and when we parted, we promised to reconnect once we got home.

Several weeks later, I reached out to Ginny. We met a few days later in a quaint coffee house. As we picked up on our conversation, we soon learned we both loved to write. Ginny suggested we meet in a month and bring back a written piece to share with one another. It had been years since I'd written and published my first book. Writer's block was an understatement but still, perhaps if I put my mind to it, the rusty gears of creativity might return.

When our next meeting time arrived, I felt a bit giddy with my newly written piece tucked into my purse. After ordering our hot tea, we found a quiet corner in the coffee shop. Exchanging our writings felt safe. There was a sense of freedom in finally getting something past my brain and onto paper. After sharing our thoughts, we agreed to meet again in a month to continue encouraging each other.

In the days that followed, God seemed to be nudging me more. I met a woman in the bookstore who wanted to start a book club. Then a very pregnant lady in the fabric store told me about a writer's group. And my sister, completely out of the blue, suggested I consider writing a non-fiction book. Then Mom reminded me of something I had written in high school.

It was my devotional that really spoke to me: *"Do not neglect the gift you have..."1 Timothy. 4:14 (ESV)* Also: *"As each has received a gift, use it to serve one another, as good stewards of God's varied grace." 1 Peter 4:10 (ESV).* I could almost hear God whispering, "Are you hearing me?" I thought of the many things I'd written that were merely files on my computer. They were of no value if they remained there. Like an "I love you" never spoken and a song never sung, if I didn't share my writing in some format, they could never bring glory to God. So, I started writing blogs as well as a novel, as my sister suggested. That book, **For The Children** was published in 2017. This book, **Awe God**, is a culmination of the blogs which reflect moments in life when God's hand was so evident, like that encounter on a plane to fan the flames to get back to writing.

So how about you? What's your gift? God gave you one to use for His honor and glory. I hope this book will serve as encouragement to get busy using and fine tuning that gift, for His glory.

Dad's Final Question

I grew up in a wonderful family where my parents farmed and raised livestock. Since they worked at home, we never had to go far to find them whenever we needed to talk or just get a hug. Mom could often be found in the sewing room, working on a new creation, and Dad, in the shop or a nearby field. They made themselves available to us to help with homework, building a parade float, or working on 4-H projects.

My grandparents were extra special; wholesome people who helped their neighbors, made room at the table for an unexpected guest, and worked hard to earn an honest living. We loved to bake cookies with Grandma. Granddad appreciated when we rubbed his back, but most fun was combing and styling his hair. He kept it longer in front and combed it back over his bald spot, but that made it great fun to put in ponytails, which he patiently tolerated. Since they lived close by, Granddad often came to our ranch to help Dad feed animals, fix a piece of equipment, or just talk while leaning over the fence.

Both Dad and Granddad believed in God, but their church meant working the land, watching the crops grow, or helping a struggling animal live. They left the spiritual side of things to the strong women in their lives. Grandma lived out her faith by serving others and her church. Mom took us to Sunday school where we learned the basics of religion, but growing up, conversations about God were reserved for mealtime grace and bedtime prayers.

Years later as a newlywed, I found myself at my dad's bedside as his five-year cancer battle neared its end. His breathing had become very labored when he asked me and my sister Colleen to sit with him a moment. He told us not to fear death. He'd seen the beautiful white light of heaven. Then he said he wanted to ask us two questions. We sat on the edge of his hospital bed that hospice brought to our home, waiting for him to catch his breath. Once he had, he asked, "Do you believe in Jesus? Really believe?" We were a bit puzzled for certainly he knew we believed; however, we assured him all the same. He didn't seem satisfied so again, asked with an urgency. Again, we assured him. Seeming satisfied, he paused to rest. Then, without getting to ask his second question, slipped into a coma. Hours later, Dad died at the age of fifty-two.

Several days later, we buried him and then attempted to move on while the void in our hearts felt as large as the man who had left it. In the days and weeks that followed, Dad's first question never left my mind. Why did he ask with such passion and intensity? I didn't understand. What about his second question, the one that never got asked? What had been left unsaid or undone?

Years went by and in time, I met the personal Jesus, not the one you just read about in Bible stories, but the One who is a friend, who wants to have a daily and intimate relationship. With new understanding, I realized why Dad asked the way he did. He wanted to know: Did we know Jesus in a personal way? It made me wonder: When did Dad meet Jesus and invite Him into his life as His personal Savior?

With new clarity on his first question, God seemed to reveal what would likely have been Dad's unasked second question. Dad would have wanted his dad, our granddad, to know Jesus too. Although Grandma had passed away, Granddad was still alive, having survived both his sons. He rarely moved from his La-Z-Boy, but he always had a smile. So, with the courage of an evangelist when sharing their faith with family, I wrote him a letter. I told Granddad about Dad's first question and his second unasked question. I shared my heart for Jesus and wrote out a prayer for him to pray. Then several weeks later, I timidly asked him if he was ready to go to heaven. He replied as a true cowboy: "Just bring me the horse."

Several years later, my beloved Granddad passed away at the age of ninety-four. I felt prompted by the Holy Spirit to speak at his funeral. Physically sick from nerves and grief, I stood at the front of the church, literally shaking as I shared my father's final question and how his unasked question prompted me to tell Granddad about Jesus. I challenged everyone in attendance to be sure of their eternal destiny by placing their faith in Christ.

The funeral ended and we gathered at the cemetery. While friends and family filed by and expressed their condolences, long-time friends Gary and Betty pulled me aside. They thanked me for sharing and then told me they had been with my dad when he accepted Jesus as his personal Savior. Several years before Dad died, Gary and Betty invited my parents to hear a Christian speaker. When an invitation for Christ was made, Dad raised his hand, accepting Jesus Christ as His Lord and Savior.

I could hardly speak as I thanked them. What a wonderful story to hear; what a blessing to finally know. Seventeen years had passed since my dad's death and I no longer needed to speculate about how or when Dad met the personal Jesus. Had I not been obedient to God and spoken at Granddad's funeral, I may never have heard the story of my dad's decision.

"Psalm 29:11 says, "The Lord gives strength to his people; the Lord blesses his people with peace." (MSG) God gave me the strength to speak at Granddad's funeral, which resulted in a blessing of peace I never expected. Today I no longer ponder Dad's first or second questions. What a blessing peace is, true peace that only comes from God.

Denise E. Johnson

Impossible Meeting

Ron and I were having dinner with a friend. We were in Southern California at the end of a long visit with her as we awaited the birth of our son. She was his birth mother and for six months, we'd planned and prepared to adopt him. She'd asked us to keep her pregnancy a secret because she never intended to tell her family. Single and ashamed of her unplanned pregnancy, she wanted to avoid the small-town gossip that would surely occur. Since my family knew her as well, we honored her request for privacy.

Our baby had taken his time though, remaining in the womb weeks past his due date. We were all getting weary as our intended week-long wait turned into nearly a month, but tomorrow, the doctor would induce labor. We decided to celebrate our last dinner together before officially becoming parents. As we sat waiting for dessert, we were stunned to see my aunt and uncle sitting just a couple tables away. They had come in after us. We hadn't noticed them, absorbed in our conversation, but they noticed us. Since no one even knew we were in California, imagine their surprise to see us there, all the way from Montana.

In shocked disbelief, we joined my aunt and uncle at their table while our friend left the restaurant, not wanting to be recognized. Seeing our own family brought such joy and relief from the stress we carried. Ron and I were homesick and exhausted from waiting. For over three weeks, we focused on providing support for our birth mother, but truth be known, we were desperately in need of support too. The weeks of waiting had taken a toll.

Then, there they were, our only family that lived in California, sitting only tables away, on the very night we were there too. We couldn't share much since we wanted to honor her secret, but having a chance to unload some of our anxieties felt like opening a backed-up dam as we cried and shared some of the stresses of the past few weeks. We didn't visit long, out of respect for our birth mother who waited in the car, but the brief visit renewed our energies, helping us feel centered again.

As we hugged them goodbye, gratitude to God filled my heart. How incredible for Him to arrange for us to be at the same restaurant, at the same time, in the same community (which wasn't the one my aunt and uncle lived in), in Southern California, on the final night before our baby would be born. The odds were impossible. *Luke 1:37* couldn't say it better: *"For with God nothing shall be impossible." (KJV)*

Denise E. Johnson

Mom's Comfort

Michael was our first child, a gift through an open adoption. We anticipated and planned for his arrival for six months. In the month we had him home, we settled into new routines and enjoyed the thrill of being parents. Michael was a beautiful, easy baby.

Over Mother's Day weekend, we took him to Helena to meet his family. We were lavished with gifts at a baby shower and announced our news of another baby coming in November. Still buoyed from the joy of the weekend, Monday arrived. When the phone rang, I was happy to hear Michael's birth mother on the other end. We were dear friends. Our conversation quickly evolved to horror as she informed me that she changed her mind and would be reclaiming Michael in two days.

As we waited, we prayed that somehow, she'd realize this abrupt change of plans was based on emotion rather than reason; that she would remember why she asked us to adopt him in the first place. We hoped our carefully planned adoption and intent for Michael's future wouldn't be discarded over an emotional reaction to Mother's Day.

Two days later, she timidly knocked on our door. Our efforts to change her mind fell on deaf ears. Her emotions overpowered her logic and she gathered our son in her arms and left. We sobbed as we watched her drive away, feeling a pain greater than any we'd ever known.

We hadn't shared her call with our family in hopes she wouldn't follow through, that she'd come to her senses and not take him from us. We hoped to shield them from the horror we were now living, but we had failed. Thus began the torturous process of calling our family and informing them Michael had been ripped from our lives. Disbelief, shock, and stunned silence were part of every conversation.

My sister and mother were most upset. They greeted us at the airport when we'd arrived home and already felt so attached to him. Mom wanted to come see us, but she had a trip coming up in a few days and couldn't take additional time off work. I tried to assure her we'd be okay. Besides, Ron decided we needed a vacation and booked a last-minute flight to Hawaii. There wouldn't be time to see Mom before we each departed for our trips.

The next few days were a blur as we dealt with our profound grief. Our home felt like a tomb, silent without the sounds of our baby, although some sounds seemed to linger, like a baby sucking on a bottle, creating a haunting eeriness. We packed with eagerness to leave the house and the memories of Michael. I called Mom as we were leaving for the airport. She was just leaving to catch her plane as well. We compared our tickets and realized that our layovers in Salt Lake City would coincide. "I'll find you at the airport," Mom promised.

Once we arrived in Salt Lake City, we made our way to our next gate. Our connection was tight and they were calling for us to board our flight. I glanced down the hallway and just then, I saw Mom, her eyes wide as she searched for us. Our eyes met and she ran toward us, her arms outstretched as if to extend a hug from the distance. Breathless, she reached us and pulled us into her, tightly embracing us as we shared our painful grief. We had less than five minutes together before our flight boarded. With one last hug, we said our goodbyes. I prayed that Mom would make her next flight as well.

God is the greatest comforter of all, but He made mothers for that very purpose too. He understood how important it was for Mom to be able to comfort us and how much we needed her comfort. So, He orchestrated our brief encounter that could only be described as providential.

Isaiah 66:13 states, "As one whom his mother comforts, so I will comfort you; you shall be comforted in Jerusalem." (ESV)

Denise E. Johnson

Humph

Humph...it doesn't seem like much of a word, but in my father's vocabulary, it had more meaning than one could imagine. Although literally a genius with a photographic memory, "humph" seemed to be how he most often expressed emotion. One would think with such intelligence, he could muster more eloquent words. Thankfully, that wasn't the only word he spoke. He spoke plenty of words of wisdom, encouragement, and correction too, but for my Dad, humph seemed the best response for those moments when words weren't quite enough. It was his unique way of expressing "I love you", "that's a good one", "I'm proud of you" and "thank you" along with a myriad of other emotions.

When we'd tell him we loved him, he had an amazing way of expressing his love with a hug and a "humph". When the fields had been harvested, "humph" showed satisfaction of a job completed. He also had a wonderful sense of humor, so on the rare occasion when we pulled a fast one on him, the "humph" said it all. When we achieved something special, the "humph" accompanied his smile of approval. Although not often enough, when we thought to thank him, his "humph" meant, "You're welcome." If we truly wanted to get his special response, we would compliment him. Humility made it difficult for him to take credit for anything, even if due.

When we raised our 4-H animals and the time came to sell them, afterwards we'd sneak off to a quiet place and cry our eyes out. Dad always found us, ready with his long arms to hug it out and let us gather ourselves. His "humph" expressed his sympathies for our loss. If we had disagreeable words and needed to make up, his "humph" affirmed "I forgive you." College meant Dad and Mom dropping us off at our dorms. A "humph" accompanied a hug and a few private tears. Then came a day when we brought home our prospective spouses for his approval. Well, you know what he said.

Perhaps Dad took *Proverbs 10:19* to heart, *"When words are many, transgression is not lacking, but whoever restrains his lips is prudent." (ESV)*. His restraint of words ensured that his words wouldn't be misunderstood or used against him. Instead, his response spoke mountains of love.

It's been decades since we heard his last "humph" and not a day goes by that we all don't miss him and his special way of expressing himself. We can't help but think of how much he would have enjoyed this season of life, watching his grandchildren graduate and move into adulthood, adding yet another generation of children to love. One thing we know for sure; with each season, each life, and each journey, he would have assured, encouraged, and cheered us on with the one word that said it all...humph!

Denise E. Johnson

Nick of Time

Nephew Sam's first birthday meant a party in Bozeman. I treasured time with my sister Colleen, so I loved this excuse to get together. Loading my toddler son Tucker into the car, we headed down the road. Colleen and I talked about days like these since we were little girls; how we'd get together with our children and make memories together. The two-hour drive flew by as I anticipated the fun day ahead.

We had barely unloaded the car when a call came from brother Dave. "Grandma had a heart attack. She's in the hospital and will go in for surgery shortly."

Scrambling to make a plan, Colleen's husband agreed to keep an eye on their three boys and Tucker so Colleen and I could make the hour and a half drive to Helena. We jumped back in the car and were on the road within moments. We hoped to get there before she went in for surgery. What if she didn't make it through? We needed to see her.

As we reached the hospital, we made haste to critical care. As we rounded the corner to the hall, Grandma was just being wheeled off to surgery. We had just caught them, without a moment to spare. The nurses paused long enough to allow us to give her a hug and tell her we loved her. Then we waited.

Grandma made it through surgery just fine. Later in the day, with Grandma safely recovering, Colleen and I drove back to Bozeman where we resumed celebrating one-year-old Sam.

The experience of that day left a huge imprint on my mind as a young mom. I realized in a new way how deeply God loved me. He knew the importance of Colleen and I seeing Grandma before her surgery. Long before any awareness of an urgent need, He attended to the details of time, distance, and companionship. Since I had already traveled the two hours to Bozeman, Colleen and I were both able to make the rest of the trip to Helena, arriving in the nick of time, allowing us to process the crisis together.

Romans 8:39 held a new perspective: *"Neither height nor depth, nor anything else in all creation, will be able to separate us from the love of God that is in Christ Jesus our Lord." (NIV)* The depths and extent of His love and compassion for us is mind-blowing. That day, I learned I could always count on God to see me through whatever life brought, and to ensure no matter the circumstance, He would provide.

Sam, please note, despite not being mentioned in my first two books, you have not only been mentioned, but given an entire chapter. Yes, I'm that great of an aunt!

Denise E. Johnson

Go After Them

Heather is like a little sister to me. As an infant, Colleen and I babysat her. When I was sixteen and Heather was five, her wonderful mother, Lana, died unexpectedly, leaving us all devastated. Our families remained close but in time, our lives went in different directions.

In spite of time and distance, Heather and I stayed in touch. With each passing year though, my concern for the direction she had taken in life heightened. When she called one day, I could hear desperation in her voice. She and her two young children were in a grave situation.

The following morning, I read Scripture from the Message translation, *"My dear friends, if you know people who have wandered off from God's truth, don't write them off. Go after them. Get them back and you will have rescued precious lives from destruction and prevented an epidemic of wandering away from God." James 5:19 (MSG)*. I felt the Holy Spirit giving me a direct order to help Heather, NOW!

So, I prayed and then went in search of a home for her young family. I found a mobile home for sale near our home. After looking it over, I decided it would be perfect. My sister and I discussed how we could help Heather purchase it, using the small inheritance that our granddad had recently left us. Then without disclosing the idea, I asked Heather to come visit me. Although I had approached her several times about moving to Billings, she had not been receptive. In light of her circumstances, perhaps she'd be open to it now.

Several weeks later, while sipping tea at my kitchen table, I shared the idea with her. We went to look at the home and when she saw it, she cried. She dreamed of this for her family. During the next few days, we checked out the school, went to church, and talked late into the night. When she left, she still hadn't made a decision. The next day she called and announced: "I'm moving to Billings." We were both giddy with excitement.

I immediately called and made an offer on the home. The next day we signed the papers. Within hours of our purchase, the realtor received two additional offers, but it was already ours. God had provided and saved it for Heather.

For the next two weeks, our family went into turbo speed, painting, cleaning, and shopping as we completed our own Home Improvement Project. Moving day arrived. When Heather pulled into her driveway, we both broke into tears. God had not only moved Heather, but impacted our hearts in profound ways as we acknowledged His hand in it all: the timing of her call, the Scripture in James, the resources from my granddad, and the perfect "fresh start" home.

In the years that followed, Heather's family flourished. She married a wonderful man and settled into the community, finding joy in her employment and growing in her walk with the Lord. Her compassion for others and faith in action has inspired me as she has "gone after others" who needed a hand up. "Rescuing precious lives from destruction" can be as simple as taking a meal, offering to watch children, shoveling a driveway, or just being a friend. God doesn't want a single one of us written off or lost. If you know someone who has wandered away, "go after them". God has a way of providing whatever is needed.

Denise E. Johnson

He Provides

The weekend promised to be so much fun as we anticipated a visit from my sister-in-law, Krista and our beloved nieces, Maria and Britney. We always had a good time when we were together. Laughter and joy filled our Friday as we played games and caught up on life. Later in the evening, we received a call that my father-in-law, Don, had been taken to the hospital. The next day, the decision was made to move him to a nursing home.

On Saturday morning, the doctor told us Don's time was short. Ron and I contacted hospice and set up a meeting for the following Monday with hopes of moving him into our home. Meanwhile, we took turns visiting Don, attending to our restaurant, and keeping an eye on our three young children.

Saturday afternoon, Ron took the kids to seven-year-old Tucker's soccer game. While there, Ron jumped up to retrieve three-year-old Kassi and wrenched his knee. He called me once he got home. He couldn't put any weight on his leg and his knee wouldn't move beyond its current position, essentially frozen. How he managed to get home with three children was miraculous.

Krista and I left Don and went home to assess the situation, which in turn meant a trip to the emergency room. After a rather long wait, we were sent home with Ron on crutches and a follow-up appointment for Monday with the Orthopedic Surgeon.

Sunday morning, Krista and the girls went to see Don but within a half-hour, drove back into our driveway. She burst out of the car with tears flowing. "Dad is failing. He's slipped into a coma." Trying to wrap our heads around the rapidly digressing situation, we all made our way to his bedside to say our final goodbyes. Since we still needed to open the restaurant the next morning, Maria went with me to get it ready.

Later that evening, with children in bed and Ron's leg propped up, Krista and I went back to be with Don. His breathing had become slow and shallow. We knew it wouldn't be long before our final goodbyes. The nurses came in to change Don's sheets, so Krista and I took a brief walk. When we returned, Don had passed away. Krista and I clutched each other in stunned shock as tears flowed. It all happened so fast.

Monday morning arrived with heaviness as we woke to the reality of our loss. Somehow in it all though, life continued. I went to open the restaurant and then hustled home to get Ron to the doctor. We learned that surgery would be needed to correct Ron's torn meniscus, but with funeral arrangements needing to be made, we decided to postpone surgery until Friday. Since Ron couldn't work, I took his place at the restaurant and left Krista and the girls in charge of the kids and Ron. It turned out to be treasured time for Ron and Krista as they processed their father's passing and made decisions together.

On Thursday Don was laid to rest. The grandchildren released balloons to symbolize sending their love to heaven with Grandpa. Then on Friday morning, we went to the hospital for Ron's surgery. Krista and the girls needed to be home since their weekend trip had stretched to a week. Since extended family had come for the funeral, they watched our children during Ron's surgery.

Our time together started out with anticipated joy, but instead became filled with multiple unplanned crises and grief. Yet, God blessed us in so many ways. Krista and the girls were here, giving them a chance to be with Don on his final weekend on earth. Ron, due to his injury, was with his family rather than working. Help to handle the restaurant and child care was available, a necessary and unexpected blessing.

Denise E. Johnson

Philippians 4:19 reminds us that *"My God will meet all your needs according to his glorious riches in Christ Jesus." (NIV)* Yes indeed, for only God could have known the need for so many details and provided for them so perfectly, making a difficult week much easier to bear.

Moving

As the overhead door to the moving van slammed down, I couldn't help but reflect on the past thirty days.

We'd been looking for a home on the west side of town for close to eight years, checking out open houses while pondering our move. With our business and church on the west end, we knew it would save us so much time and gas if we could move closer. I contacted my realtor friend Helen and off we went house hunting. We'd been at it for a couple weeks when we drove into a neighborhood I'd always liked. As we pulled into the driveway of the listed home, I let out a gasp. I'd fallen in love with this house two years earlier.

Back then, it was still under construction, but even so, I'd pulled into the driveway and made my way into the house. Stepping over plywood floor boards and weaving between wall studs to reach the construction workers, I inquired about the house. I remember my disappointment in learning they were building it for a family, thus already sold.

Two years later, here we were, seeing this beautifully finished and completely landscaped home. As we wandered through it, I felt ecstatic. It met all our criteria, in a cul-de-sac, in a rural school district, with enough bedrooms for each child, a big backyard for the kids to play, and only two years old, thus not needing repairs or upgrades. Sold!

Since Ron and I were running a restaurant, we couldn't get away to look at it together, so Ron went to see it with Helen a few days later. Upon his approval, I went back to see it one more time. Then we made the offer.

There was a hitch though. The seller wouldn't take a contingency and since we hadn't even listed our house yet, we ran the risk of having two house payments. Back and forth we went with offers until finally, we agreed to drop the contingency and prayed we'd find a buyer on our current home. Later that day Helen called. The listing realtor on our new house knew someone who wanted a house similar to our existing home. Could they come look at it today?

For the next few hours, we scrambled to make the house company clean and then loaded our three children into the car. As I pulled the door shut behind me, I glanced around, making sure everything was in order and then whispered a prayer: "Lord, let them want the house and the refrigerator." The new house had white appliances, not almond like our current refrigerator. It seemed a silly detail, but one that needed to be addressed.

Several hours later, we arrived back home. Within minutes, Helen called. "They are going to make a full-price offer!" Excited doesn't begin to describe how we felt. She asked me a few questions about the sprinkler system and central air. Content with the answers, she stated, "Great, we should have the offer later today." I was just about to hang up the phone when she called out, "Oh, Denise. I forgot to ask. They wondered if you'd be willing to leave the refrigerator?" Tears sprung to my eyes. "Yes, of course."

Psalm 20:4 says, "May he give you the desire of your heart and make all your plans succeed." (NIV)

After years of searching, in a mere thirty-day whirlwind, we'd found our new home, negotiated a price, sold our home without even listing it, closed on both homes, and moved. If we ever doubted that God was behind the details and our plans to move, we simply thought about the refrigerator, the only thing that didn't make the move with us.

The Strike

Our community boiled over with controversy. Families were split as sides were taken. The teachers planned to strike if wage requests weren't met. As the school board prepared for a potential strike, they asked people to step up as substitute teachers. Although I respected the teachers' position, I couldn't help but worry about the students. I knew there would be parents who could not afford to miss work to stay home with their children. Some children could be left unsupervised if parents were forced to make difficult decisions.

Ron and I talked about it. Since our children were attending school out of the district, they wouldn't be affected by the strike. We had just moved to this rural school district and with Kassi starting kindergarten and Tucker in fourth grade, I was grateful their schooling wouldn't be disrupted by the strike. Daycare could be arranged for Josh so I decided to apply.

We heard rumors of how badly the substitute teachers would be treated by the striking personnel. I wasn't one to look for a fight but again, what about the children? I could support the children by making sure they had a safe place to go while the adults worked out their differences. Perhaps the striking teachers wouldn't see it that way, but God put it upon my heart to help the children.

The rumors were true. From the moment I went to apply for the position at the administrative building, striking teachers confronted me, trying to dissuade me. My devotion that morning encouraged me: *1 Corinthians 4:12-13a, "When we are cursed, we bless; when we are persecuted, we endure it, when we are slandered, we answer kindly." (NIV)*

So, with scripture in mind, I pushed on. Arriving at my assigned school on the first day, I quietly made my way past a small group of striking teachers who cast glares my way. Inside, Tina became my team leader as we attended to the children. She wasn't a union employee, so she risked being fired if she didn't work. She needed to provide for her family, but it also concerned her, knowing she would eventually work with teachers who might not appreciate her decision.

Tina and I settled into a routine. Daily we crossed the picket line and took care of children whose parents needed the support of the school. God continued to encourage me through Scriptures: *1 Corinthians 7:15: "God has called us to live in peace." (NIV)*. So, I walked with my head up, knowing I was serving as God intended.

As the days passed, the hostility became more intense. One afternoon, I walked to my vehicle and as I closed my door, a man came right up to my driver's side window and angrily shouted at me. I managed to get out of the parking lot, but it rattled and frightened me, particularly as I heard of threats, including a school board member who had been run off the road and injured. I questioned if I should continue.

Every morning, God gave me a new Scripture to ponder: *1 Corinthians 9:12 "We put up with anything rather than hinder the gospel of Christ." (NIV) "Do not be afraid, for not one of you will fall apart from the will of your Father. So do not be afraid."*

Matthew 10:28 & 29b (NIV) When I began to falter in my resolve, he gave me this word in *1 Corinthians 16:8-9 "For the present, I'm staying right here. A huge door of opportunity for good work has opened up here. There is also mushrooming opposition. (MSG)"* So, I stayed until the teacher strike ended.

It was a season of trusting God as He trained and taught me that in all circumstances, it is my job to reflect His peace and love so that His work can be done, even if others don't agree.

Awe God

A Chinese Bible

With Christmas fast approaching, I often think of my second favorite Christmas story. It happened years ago when we owned a restaurant. Nine-year-old son Tucker, had a special relationship with our cooks, Sam and Caroline, a couple from China. About ten days before Christmas, Tucker told me he wanted to buy them a Bible for Christmas, not just any Bible, a Chinese Bible. I couldn't imagine where we'd find a Chinese Bible in Montana, let alone just days before Christmas.

    We decided to try, so we searched the Christian stores and on-line stores, but to no avail. As the days ticked by, it didn't look like we were going to find one. Perhaps we'd have to settle for an English Bible, but then I thought of how our local radio station advertised purchasing Bibles for China through the Bible League. Maybe they could connect us with the Bible League to purchase one, even if we couldn't get it in time for Christmas.

    I made the call to the radio station and shared our mission. The receptionist became very quiet and then, almost in a whisper, said, "We have a Chinese Bible here. We've been praying for a family who could use it. You can just have this one!" We were stunned. Tucker and I immediately jumped in the car and drove to the radio station to pick it up. Tucker then carefully wrapped the beautiful leather burgundy Bible, excited to have his special gift for Sam and Caroline.

    When Christmas Eve arrived, we took Sam and Caroline to church with us. They sat with eyes wide with wonder as they watched the service and listened to the music. Then we took them for a drive to look at Christmas lights. Once we got back to their apartment, we unloaded the back of the van which contained a small living tree and a few decorations. As they watched with wide grins, we decorated their tree and then placed a few packages under it. The final touch was a small nativity scene which we put on their mantle. All the while, Sam asked questions about the Christmas traditions we were sharing.

Tucker then pulled out his special gift and gave it to Caroline, asking her to open it. When she did, she began chattering excitedly in Chinese as she showed Sam their gift. Tears were in her eyes as she gushed over Tucker, thanking him over and over again. She couldn't believe we found a Chinese Bible. As the evening came to a close, we sang them Christmas carols and then departed, instructing them to wait until morning to open their presents. Just as we left, Sam said, "Now we know what Christmas is."

VERY EARLY Christmas morning our phone rang. It was Sam. He sounded as excited as a child as he thanked us for his gifts. Caroline later confided that Sam hardly slept, anxious for morning to arrive so he could open the packages.

Years have passed since Sam and Caroline were in our lives. Last we'd heard, they moved back to China. In a country where Christians are persecuted for having a Bible, I can only wonder what happened to their Bible. I trust it is still blessing others since God went to such great lengths to place a Chinese Bible in Billings, Montana just days before Christmas, so Tucker could give his special gift to our friends.

Since receiving our Christmas miracle of the Chinese Bible, I treasure my own Bible even more. I am so blessed to have one and be able to read it whenever I want. I don't have to hide it or worry about being punished or killed for having it. Perhaps one day, God will allow us to see the fruits of that one Chinese Bible. Until then, I hope I never take for granted the opportunity to spend time in God's word. Regardless of what language it is written in, it is a gift from God, much like the gift of His son, which by the way, is my favorite Christmas story.

Waiting for Baily

She was our first child. Okay, so actually, our first pet. We picked Angel out as a puppy; a beautiful golden retriever. She would be a great family dog when we finally had children.

Initially, Angel became attached to Ron, following him closely. Several years later, after months of bed rest while waiting for Tucker's birth, she became my dog, never leaving my side. When Tucker arrived, Angel loved him, attentive to every cry, licking his feet should they ever poke out from his sleeper. Over time, our boy and his dog became inseparable.

After sixteen years, Angel began to fail. She struggled to get up the stairs and lost bladder control. One day she tumbled down the stairs and when I rushed to her, her eyes said it all. Her time with us was coming to an end.

When the kids came home after school, we had to tell them that our Angel passed away. Tucker cried the most as he recalled how he'd prayed to God that Angel would be there when he got home. Angel constantly shed hair, so Tucker quietly gathered up patches and presented them to me. "Please put these in a safe place so I can always remember her."

The weeks that followed seemed very empty without our beloved Angel. Soon, Tucker began asking for a new puppy. He went online and looked over different breeds. Finally, he decided he'd like a female English Springer Spaniel and asked if we could get one.

We told him he'd need to wait until summer break as it would give him time to train her, but he simply couldn't wait that long. Many times, when we took our evening walk, he would beg me to let him have a puppy. Then he'd resort to, "You're never going to let me have a puppy!"

I tried to encourage him to wait on God's perfect timing, reminding him the right puppy would come at the right time. Determined, Tucker remained persistent as he scoured the newspapers. As time passed and he saw no ads for Springer Spaniels, he decided he'd be happy with another breed, just so he could get it soon. We held fast, insisting he must wait for school to break for summer.

Spring dragged by as Tucker attempted to cajole us. Then, about two weeks before summer break, he noticed an ad for two female English Springer Spaniels! We made the call and much to our relief, one of the female pups was still available, liver and white colored just like Tucker wanted.

Since the puppy was out of town, we discussed how to get her. They mentioned they planned to come to town soon and would call when they could confirm the date. A week later they asked if we could meet them the following Saturday, the day after school got out for the summer.

With the money he had saved clutched in his hand, Tucker and his dad waited patiently in the Shopko parking lot. Bailey instantly won our hearts and became a treasured member of the family. In the Message translation, *Habakkuk 2:3 states, "If it seems slow in coming, wait. It's on its way. It will come right on time." (MSG)* What a perfect description of what God taught us as we waited for Tucker's perfect puppy. Wait for it; wait for it; wait for it! It's worth the wait when it comes in God's time.

A Part-time Job

One year Ron and I decided that since we were self-employed, one of us needed to get a part-time job for insurance benefits. Since I didn't want to run our restaurant alone, I volunteered. After all, I could certainly squeeze a part-time job into raising three children, maintaining our home, keeping the restaurant books and employee schedules, volunteering at school, keeping up with the kids' extra-curricular activities and oh, how could I forget, be a wife! I could probably even cover a shift now and then at the restaurant if needed.

So off I went job hunting, and of course, landed the one job I never wanted to have, a bank teller. Not that there's anything wrong with being a teller. It's just that I hate to count money and I'm self-conscious about my hands since I'm a nailbiter, but it would work into our part-time plan. Before you think we pulled this off, let me assure you that nine months into this, I informed Ron he could either buy me a straight-jacket or a coffin, because I'd need one or the other SOON!

Back to my story. One day as the bank opened, a rather large line of customers began to form. Everyone seemed to be impatient as they shot urgent stares at us. As I glanced at the line, I noticed a woman several people back who looked particularly upset. As I finished with my customer, I glanced up and realized the woman that looked upset was going to be my next customer. I felt dread and braced myself for what I expected to be a raging complaint. Greeting her, I began to process her transaction.

Suddenly, she began crying.

"Are you okay?" I asked.

"No," she said, "I just got word my grandson died."

Instinctively I reached out and covered her hand with mine, expressing my sorrow while struggling to keep my own emotions in check. Her story came spilling out as she told me her six-month-old grandson had died that morning, most likely from Sudden Infant Death Syndrome (SIDS). She needed to cash a check before she left town to be with her daughter. I cashed her check and as I handed her the cash, I squeezed her hand again, stating that I would be praying for her and her family. She graciously thanked me and left.

As she left, I stepped away for a moment to gather myself. Stunned at what just happened, I stopped to assess the situation. There were four of us in the teller windows that day, one expecting her first child, another who wasn't a Christian, the other, a young man. Had that grandmother shared her story with any of the other tellers, it might have been frightening or very uncomfortable. Instead, God had maneuvered her to my window, someone who had lost a baby, who understood the loss and pain of SIDS. In my very ordinary part-time job, God allowed me to minister to this grieving grandmother. Maybe that is the only reason I worked for nine months as a teller.

In *2 Corinthians 1:4: "He comforts us in all our troubles so that we can comfort others. When they are troubled, we will be able to give them the same comfort God has given us." (NIV)*

Although I offered compassion and comfort that day, God showed me that my losses could be used to help and comfort others, even in a teller line.

Be a Container

As I looked at myself in the mirror, I realized I wouldn't be going to work. We ran a restaurant and in my role as cashier and server, I couldn't go in with my face looking like this. A red welt with seeping pus covered my left side, and it felt like it was on fire. Pretty, right? I made my way to the doctor who took one look at me and gasped. She diagnosed me with shingles along with an active staph infection.

In the months that followed, even as my infection cleared, my fatigue worsened, leaving me doing little more than holding down the couch. Then I developed a tremor. Multiple specialists tried to determine the cause, but there were no answers. Meanwhile, Ron covered the demands of the restaurant while balancing home and school events for the kids.

Months into my undiagnosed tremor, after a spinal tap, I needed to lie flat for several hours after the procedure. Ron called from the store. His frustration and fatigue came through in his voice. One of the employees had called off and now they were short-handed. He knew I couldn't help. He just needed to vent. After the call, as I continued to lay on the couch, I felt angry and disappointed I couldn't be where I needed to be. In full transparency, I was angry at God too. How could I be stuck here when Ron needed me elsewhere?

Wallowing in my own self-pity, I received another call. Dear friends asked if they could stop over for a visit. Well, I wasn't going anywhere so, why not? When they arrived, they shared a crisis going on in their lives. We talked for over an hour and then we prayed.

When they left, they seemed more at peace as they thanked me for being there for them.

In the quiet of my home, still planted flat on my back on the couch, I apologized to God, recognizing I was exactly where He needed and wanted me to be. The restaurant survived another day without me, but I'm not so sure my friends would have made it without a reminder of God's goodness, and His power to overcome life's obstacles. It was a lesson I needed to learn that day as well.

God placed me exactly where I needed to be. Had I not been confined to my couch; I'd have rushed off to work to cover that shift and missed God's important assignment. He reminded me that no matter where we are, He can use us in the circumstances of the day, if only we take our eyes off ourselves and look to His purpose and plan.

In the Message translation, *2 Timothy 2:20-21* reads: *"In a well-furnished kitchen there are some containers used to serve fine meals, others to take out the garbage. Become the kind of container God can use to present any and every kind of gift to his guests for their blessing."*

What a blessing to be used in the manner He deems necessary.

Seven Long Years

How did a Scandinavian couple end up running a fast-food Japanese restaurant? Interesting question: One we'd been asked at least a hundred times. The answer was equally interesting. It started out with the best intentions. A nice young man whom we considered a friend approached Ron about being a silent partner in his restaurant venture. He wanted to go out on his own. It appeared to be a great way to diversify and do something fun.

However, the nice young man turned out to be a crook and no matter how hard we worked to come to a resolution, we ended up in court. The judge ruled in our favor and awarded us the restaurant. But wait. Wait! Neither of us had ever worked in a restaurant nor had a desire to own or manage one. We just wanted our money back, or at least some of it.

When life gives you lemons, you make lemonade, or in our case, teriyaki sauce! With the keys in our hands, we realized that if we were ever going to get our investment back, we'd need to run the business ourselves. Perhaps after a couple good years of clean books, we could sell it and put this restaurant chapter in the rear-view mirror.

Those couple of years toiled into seven long years as we kept looking for a buyer. Unlike a job, you can't just quit a business when you're ready to be done. In all honesty though, it was a worthwhile experience in many ways. We met some wonderful friends and used our Japanese restaurant as our mission field, playing Christian music on the radio and loving on those who came through the door.

Exhaustion had taken its toll though, especially with three young children and no family in town to support us. We'd juggled sick children, missed birthday parties, passed each other as we changed shifts, and endured the physical strain of keeping a business healthy. We never intended to run the restaurant this long and both of us were ready for a change. Out of the blue, after seven long years, we received an offer to buy the restaurant. That left us wondering, what's next Lord?

With the closing date locked in, Ron went looking for a job. Several interviews later, we were still searching. Then, on the exact day we closed on the sale of the restaurant, a job offer came through for Ron. Seven long years of waiting and it all changed on the exact same day!

Our wait that concluded after seven long years caused me to think of *Deuteronomy 15:1-2: "At the end of every seven years you shall grant a release. And this is the manner of the release; every creditor shall release what he has lent to his neighbor. He shall not exact it of his neighbor, his brother, because the Lord's release has been proclaimed." (ESV)*

Clearly, we weren't in financial bondage like described in the Old Testament, but boy did we ever have a sense of what being "released" felt like. The relief that came, knowing we'd done our best to put the restaurant back on firm footing, to serve our customers and staff well, and to now move onto a new chapter with a clean conscience.

What a great reminder to not hold onto anything too long, whether it is a business or job that you aren't passionate about, a grudge against another, or a debt owed. Although we were never fully compensated for the theft by our deceptive partner, God gave us a season of good, honest work to make some great friends, and a reason to better understand the value of His release. Life is much too short to let our burdens linger. Perhaps there are things that you need to release and move beyond too.

Perseverance

All summer long, our daughter and I talked of her trying out for the swim team. Actually, that's not true. Kassi wanted to try-out for years, but with our restaurant, we couldn't make commitments that would take us away on the weekends. Now that we'd sold the restaurant, we could finally pursue other interests.

  I made some calls and talked to someone in charge of the swim team. Try-outs would be the second week in September and someone would be in touch with further details. However, just in case we didn't hear anything, they suggested we call the Sunday prior to try-outs. I put it on the calendar and when that Sunday arrived, I made the call. Imagine our disappointment to be told the try-outs occurred the previous week. Selections had been made. It was too late.

  Kassi's disappointment crushed me. I felt horrible. To make matters worse, we hadn't signed up for any other sports because we thought she'd be swimming. Soccer and basketball seasons were well underway, thus too late for Kassi to participate. Knowing I needed to keep my darling busy, I agreed to let her do gymnastics, a sport she loved in her earlier years. The alternative plan thrilled her and within the week, she had moved up to the next level.

  As I watched her from the waiting room, I recognized an acquaintance whose daughter was also in the program. As we visited, my friend mentioned her daughter had recently joined the swim team. My ears perked up and I shared our disappointment in missing try-outs. My friend suggested we show up at swimming practice with Kassi in a swimsuit and tell our sad story of how we'd missed out on the try-outs.

So, the following day, that's exactly what we did. Initially the coach expressed reluctance, stating they already had more kids swimming than they could handle. We remained steadfast and they eventually allowed Kassi to swim. As she made her way down the pool, I sat watching her from the bench. In her typical competitive spirit, she started passing other more experienced swimmers in the pool. After an hour and a half of this, the coach invited Kassi to join the team. We were so ecstatic.

Kassi worked hard, even getting herself out of bed for early morning practices. Two months later, Kassi's times were fast enough to compete at the State meet in five different events. By the end of the season, she was recognized as "most improved swimmer".

What an amazing God to align an old friend at a mutual location at just the right time so our daughter could find joy in swimming. In the process, Kassi learned an important lesson in the value of persevering.

Romans 5:3-4: "We rejoice in our sufferings, knowing that suffering produces perseverance, and perseverance produces character, and character produces hope." (ESV)

The Perfect Job

I loved my job as the Volunteer/Marketing Coordinator at the preschool. From day one, I stretched to learn new tasks and skills. With each day, I fully acknowledged I could only succeed with God's help. In time, I mastered new skills and developed great friendships with the staff, putting out professional quality newsletters and making contacts with the media and public. I flourished in my job and the Director, my supervisor, loved my work and the outcomes of it.

During my third year there, my respect for my supervisor waned as I observed some of her decisions. Then she and I had a major disagreement. As the volunteer coordinator, I screened and conducted background checks on volunteers who worked in the classrooms. When I learned that some parents hadn't been screened, I pulled them aside and ran background checks. In the process, I learned one parent was a registered sex offender. When I brought this to my supervisor's attention, she informed me the parent had been cleared by her, even knowing this detail. I couldn't believe it, so I brought the issue to the attention of the management team and the Human Resources Director who all agreed; the parent couldn't continue to volunteer with the children.

As I attempted to convince my supervisor of the dangers of the parent volunteer being a registered sex offender, our relationship digressed. She began treating me with hostility. When my evaluation came up, instead of the high marks I previously received, she gave me lots of criticism and low scores. I anguished about how to handle these conflicts. I lost sleep trying to figure out what to do and prayed for answers. One night I woke abruptly and I heard the still small voice of God, "Who will fight for the kids if you don't?" I realized I needed to escalate this issue to the Board. In doing so, I knew I'd have to resign as her hostility would only increase once I escalated the issue. It broke my heart. I loved this job and I had become very good at it, thanks to many co-workers and God's divine hand.

With a heavy heart, in preparation for the next board meeting, I wrote my resignation letter and gathered the evidence of the volunteer parent. I admired many of the members of the board and wanted them to hear the facts directly from me as well as my reason for resigning.

As I sat through the meeting, waiting for my opportunity to speak, I felt ill with nerves. I had never had to leave a job under such negative circumstances nor been in a position where I had to speak against my boss. When my opportunity to speak came, I shared my news. The room fell into a silent state of shock. Before I left, several board members thanked me for the job I'd done and expressed their sadness in my decision to resign. All the way home, I trembled and cried, grieving the difficult decision I'd been forced to make, yet relieved, knowing I'd made the right choice.

I needed to do one more thing: I wrote a letter to the County Attorney, pointing out the lack of protections from registered sex offenders in schools. During the next legislative session, a bill was brought forth to block these offenders from schools and signed into law.

God gave me the perfect job; it just wasn't the job I thought. Generating reports, training volunteers, or interacting with staff laid the groundwork necessary to be able to see a much bigger issue: one that put all children in Montana at risk. If it hadn't been for my perfect job, I wouldn't have known about this horrific gap in protections for children. God put me where I needed to be, as I'm sure He's put you exactly where you need to be as well. Take advantage of that and use it to serve God.

Esther 4:14: "For if you remain silent at this time...and who knows that you have come to this royal position for such a time as this?" (NIV)

Wanted: Wisdom

Ever have one of those days when you miss those you've lost? I was having one of those days, thinking of my dad. He died way too young at the age of fifty-two from colon cancer. Even though it had been years since he'd passed, I couldn't stop thinking about him, perhaps because I'd just turned fifty-two. I had outlived my father's age. He seemed so much more mature and confident than I felt. On the other hand, I'm pretty sure I look younger at fifty-two than he did. That's another subject that probably should go under the title of "Denial".

Anyway, back to my point: I missed Dad. In the decades since he'd passed, I felt his absence most when I wanted his advice. Funny how we don't appreciate our parents' advice while they're willing and able to share it, especially when we're teenagers. Although there were many wise people in my life, including my mom, sometimes I just wanted to talk to Dad. What I would have given to have his input when we were forced to relinquish our first son after our adoption fell apart or when our business partner embezzled our sizable investment. How I wish I could have discussed whether I should leave my job after my boss and I had ethical differences. I missed him the most as my children were growing up. How I would have appreciated his wise, fatherly counsel and his light-hearted wit. If only he had lived long enough to meet his grandchildren. He would have been so proud of them, and they would have been blessed by his wisdom and involvement in their lives.

My house felt quieter than usual, making Dad's absence seem larger. With the boys in school and Kassi away on her eighth-grade class trip, I realized they were growing up fast.

The pinging sound of my cell phone interrupted my thoughts. As I looked at my phone, I noticed a text message from Kassi. A smile crossed my face. Perhaps she missed me as much as I missed her. Before I could read the message, an image popped up. I caught my breath. She had sent me a picture, a picture of my dad. Then another picture followed, one of our family when we were much younger.

Tears welled up in my eyes as I sent her back a message, "Where did you see these pictures?"

"At the Little Red School House! We camped overnight here last night."

The Little Red School House in Helena had been renovated as a historic site. My grandparents and parents had been actively involved in the restoration project. Evidently, as a way to recognize those families who had helped, pictures had been mounted on the wall, including one of Dad and our family. I had no idea the pictures were there. What a wonderful surprise.

I felt like I had just been given a hug from God. In His wondrous way, He had used technology and my daughter's class trip to give me the gift of "seeing" Dad. Although I couldn't have a conversation with my wise dad, my wise Father, who is just a prayer away, knew the longings of my heart.

Psalm 37:4 "Delight yourself in the LORD, and he will give you the desires of your heart." (NIV)

James 1:5-6: "If any of you lacks wisdom, let him ask God, who gives generously to all without reproach, and it will be given him. But let him ask in faith, with no doubting, for the one who doubts is like a wave of the sea that is driven and tossed by the wind." (ESV)

What Divides Us

My son Josh and I were reading his nightly devotional about divisions in the church, and how they are often a result of how we judge one another or our motives. As we were reading, it seemed very timely considering the upcoming national elections and the divisiveness in our country.

As we finished the devotional, I felt a nudge from God, the one I often do when He inspires me to write. The devotional reminded me that no matter who the candidates are or which political party we think is to blame for our circumstances, the real culprit is Satan. The enemy loves it when families are fighting across the dinner table. He loves when neighbors stop talking to each other and when the word "hate" is spewed across the internet. He really enjoys any hold he has on our lives because he's the master of hate and division. However, that doesn't mean we have to take his bait. It is still our personal choice as to whether we'll go along with his lies and manipulation.

James 3:17-18 is full of truth: *"Real wisdom, God's wisdom, begins with a holy life and is characterized by getting along with others."* Do you think James meant this for times like these? That we should get along regardless of whether we're Republicans or Democrats, regardless of who gets elected? I believe so.

James' counsel isn't done as he continues in chapter 4:1-3: *"Where do you think all these appalling wars and quarrels come from? Do you think they just happen? Think again. They come about because you want your own way, and fight for it deep inside yourselves. You lust for what you don't have and are willing to kill to get it. You want what isn't yours and will risk violence to get your hands on it." (MSG)*

In this time of so much strife and division, there couldn't be a greater need for Christians to be the hands and feet of Christ, being salt and light in a world of turmoil. No matter who wins politically, there will be so many who feel defeated after a hard-fought battle.

Regardless of the outcome, I have determined I will not wring my hands in despair nor arrogantly proclaim a victory, but rather trust that God allowed it. Since He allowed it, I will, to the best of my ability, love people, share His Message, and present peace and unity because strife, discord, and judgment will only divide us further.

Let's all give each other a break and recognize the enemy doesn't deserve a place in our lives. Let's decide now to not allow Satan to take hold of our emotions or let our fears become our actions. Instead, let's live humbly and in peace with one another, respecting each other's opinions without judging, and focusing on what unites us rather than what divides us. Let's truly honor God, regardless of who wins this election.

God Bless the United States of America.

Help Wanted

We were just entering the church sanctuary when I heard the usher speak into her radio. "A kid just threw up. I'm going to need some help."

It caused me to do an about face and head out to the foyer. Yes indeed, the morning hadn't started out well. We were running late for church which of course meant conversation with the children regarding responsibilities and timeliness. Once we got to the church parking lot, there wasn't a spot anywhere close, so we ended up walking a longer distance than usual which, MIND YOU, made us even later!

We are creatures of habit and sit in the same section of the sanctuary every week, but when I heard the usher's words, it seemed like a good time to move to a new section. As a good Christian parent, I know my first thought should have been to pray for that child and his family, but no, in complete transparency, my only thought was, "We are NOT sitting here, in our usual section." In one quick movement, I halted my crew at the door and did my best to steer them into another section. They all stared at me with baffled expressions that seemed to reflect, "Mom has completely lost it!" Since church had already started, once we were settled in our new section, I whispered the details to them. Their faces relaxed into expressions of understanding and relief.

It felt a bit awkward viewing the service from another location, but overall, the sermon was uneventful, except for the woman who arrived even later (imagine that!!!) and squeezed herself into a seat in the middle of the row. Something about her seemed off, so I kept glancing at her.

As church concluded, the pews emptied, but the single woman remained in her seat, and then slipped to her knees in an almost upright fetal position. I waited until everyone else left, and then moved over to join her. As I put my hand on her shoulder, she lifted her head with tear-filled eyes.

"Can I help you?" I asked. She poured out her heart, sharing the sadness bottled inside. We visited and prayed together until she had gathered her emotions. I offered to meet her for coffee and shared resources available at the church. After about ten minutes, we hugged each other and parted ways.

I never heard from her again, but the impact she had on me was much greater than any I could have had on her. It created one of those memories that sticks with you and resurfaces at random times, and when it does, I pause to pray for her.

What started off as a morning completely off track, ended up resulting in a cascade of lessons. Had we not been THAT late, we might have been the recipient of someone's reverse breakfast. Had we not been THAT late, we might have missed sitting in the same row as a hurting young woman and thus, missed the privilege of praying with her. Finally, had we been in a hurry to hustle out of church and onto our next event of the day, we would surely have missed this woman's need to be comforted.

God knows when and how things should unfold. Sometimes He gives us the most unusual signals, if only we are paying attention. Help was wanted on many levels that morning. If it took a child throwing up in church to plant me in a section where I could help comfort one of His lost, well, it just doesn't get more creative than that, but why should that be a surprise? He is, after all, the God of creation. *Genesis 1:1 "First this: God created the Heavens and Earth—all you see, all you don't see." (MSG)*

To Africa

When our daughter Kassi was thirteen, she mentioned that she wanted to go to Africa to tell orphans about God. Her request surprised me but also sparked my long-ago dream of serving in an orphanage. Amid raising a family and running a business, life had squeezed out such dreams. Since our family had a habit of putting goals in my red leather journal, Kassi and I wrote, "Go to Africa" in the journal. Even as I wrote it out, I couldn't imagine it happening.

Months later while reading the church bulletin, I read a notification looking for volunteers to go to Africa on a short-term mission trip to serve in an orphanage. A chill ran down my back and without saying a word, I passed the bulletin to Kassi, pointing at the notice. Her eyes popped wide. "Mom, we're going!"

A few weeks later we attended the orientation meeting and filled out the application. Then word came that we'd been accepted to be part of the team. We were so excited, but also nervous. Could I seriously be taking my young daughter to the other side of the ocean to a third world country? With everything going on in the world? We plowed ahead as I reminded myself that God opened the door. We raised money, got passports, and obtained the required vaccinations.

Frustration and doubts rose as the trip got rescheduled three times. With the trip finally locked in for the fall, we made arrangements for Kassi to be gone from school and me from work. The day of our trip arrived. We couldn't have been more excited nor nervous. I also struggled with being a bit afraid. Most of my fears revolved around the huge responsibility of having Kassi with me. What if I lost her somewhere or she was taken from me? What if she got sick or needed medical care? The what-ifs seemed to multiply. At the same time, I hoped it would be a special time of bonding.

After a tremendously long flight, we had a fast layover in London where we ate fish and chips and literally ran from one famous sight to the next. Then onto Addis Ababa, Ethiopia where the contrast couldn't have been more dramatic. Poverty, homelessness, and children wandering the streets unattended. The gravity of need felt immense.

Leaving Addis, we headed to Guder where we would be staying while serving New Hope Orphanage. That trip created white knuckles while we clutched our seats as the driver swerved the bus around people and animals on the road, using his blaring horn more than his brake.

Arriving at the orphanage, we were greeted with smiling, happy children. They sang and adorned us with flowers and hugs as we got off the bus. I don't think I've cried that many happy tears in my life. We were so moved.

For ten days, we built a tower for a gravity-flow water system. Kassi seemed to become a new person without the distractions of her cell phone and barrage of peer pressures, like watching a rose bud come into full bloom. The children hung on her and were constantly at her side. I knew she had always been a kid-magnet, but wow, these little brown children just adored her, braiding her hair and lavishing her with their love.

Time flew and before we knew it, we needed to say goodbye. Exhausted from hard work and emotional connections made with the children, we departed, leaving half our hearts with the beautiful African children.

An impossible goal, written in a journal at precisely the right time, became an incredible experience. We only hoped someday we could return to the children we'd come to love as our own. Our lives would never be the same! In this special journey, I learned that no matter where I am with, or without my daughter, *"The Lord will keep you from all harm. He will watch over your life. The Lord will watch over your coming and going, both now and forevermore." Psalm 121: 7-8 (NIV)*

The Orphans

He couldn't have been more than five. His eyes were shy, as if seeking an invitation. When I extended my hand, inviting him to take it, a smile spread across his face, revealing a toothless grin. He scurried across the dusty road and took my outstretched hand. As his hand slipped into mine, I looked down at his beautiful little brown hand, tightly squeezing mine. He looked up at me as if he had just won the lottery.

We were walking among the orphans in Ethiopia. Dust kicked up as we walked. The streets were full of noise and yet, we walked in silence, not having a language to share. Still, I could feel a bond between us.

He held on tightly, not wanting to relinquish my hand to another child who attempted to get close. There were so many children scampering along beside us. I doubted any of them had a home to call their own, perhaps not even a mama or daddy to watch over them.

As I surveyed him, I noticed he wasn't wearing shoes, just like most of the children in the streets. I stooped to get at his level. His face was smudged with dirt, but his smile was as big as the sunshine.

Looking around, my heart felt full. A thought crossed my mind: "Who does this? Who gets this amazing opportunity to walk among these beautiful people who have nothing to give but their smile?" The answer came quickly. "You do, not because you're special, but because when you were called, you came."

I couldn't help but smile. I was the last person on the face of the earth who ever expected to travel across the globe, especially to

Africa. I loved being at home, a homebody, not a missionary. I liked the safety of familiarity, not the unknown of a strange culture, yet here I was. I was overwhelmed with the privilege.

As we reached our hotel, I let go of the hand of the little lad who had accompanied me down the street. I leaned down to give him a kiss on his dirty little face. "Jesus loves you," I told him, even though I knew he didn't understand. Perhaps God, in his grace, allowed my words to be heard in his own language. With that, he ran off, a beaming smile across his face.

I never knew his name. I will never see him again, but my heart remains full of love for him, just as it is for many of the people I met in Ethiopia. Walking on a dusty road in Ethiopia among the orphans was nothing short of a gift from God, and I will forever be changed.

"Religion that God our Father accepts as pure and faultless is this: to look after orphans and widows in their distress and to keep oneself from being polluted by the world." James 1:27 (NIV)

Back to Africa

We had fallen in love with Africa and the beautiful children at New Hope. Not a day passed when they weren't on our minds and in our prayers. Our longing to go back seemed to be all we could think about. Kassi never wasted an opportunity to remind me that she really, REALLY wanted to return to Africa. When the church bulletin again advertised for a short-term mission team the following year, my heart quickened. Perhaps we could go again? I didn't say anything to Kassi, not yet. With Kassi starting high school, I needed to check with the administrator to make sure she could miss that much time from school. Besides, it would be hard to fund it so soon after the last trip. Then again, with passports and immunizations done, we wouldn't have those costs.

The orientation meeting for the trip took place when Kassi was out of town at the State Swim meet, so with Ron and her gone, I slipped off to the meeting and filled out the paperwork for both of us, all without Kassi's knowledge. I prayed, knowing if we were supposed to go again, God would make it clear. Next, I began plotting how to break the news to Kassi.

The opportunity came along about a month later. The local Exchange Club asked us to share about our trip to Africa. With as much cooperation as possible between mother and teenage daughter, we managed to pull together a PowerPoint presentation. When we got to the meeting, I intended to prompt a friend to ask: "Are you going to go back to Africa?" This would give me the opportunity to surprise Kassi.

Arriving at the room, we realized the short power cord meant pulling the projector back, resulting in the pictures being too small to see on the opposite wall. The presentation didn't go smoothly; we should have practiced more. Adding to my stress was the realization that my friend didn't show up, so I didn't get to plant the question.

When we finished our presentation, the audience asked questions. Kassi answered them with passion and enthusiasm, and as she did, my mind whirled trying to come up with Plan B to launch the surprise. When the host gave the opportunity for one more question, my heart sank. I hadn't figured out Plan B yet. A woman raised her hand. "Do you plan to go back?" Tears welled up in my eyes.

Kassi answered, "Yes, definitely, right Mom?" I smiled at her and then, choking back emotion, added, "I am so glad you asked that question because what Kassi doesn't know is we are going back in October." Kassi's jaw dropped open as tears rolled down her cheeks. "Are you serious, Mom?" Like any good mother, I started crying too. Yep, right there in front of everyone, we put on a waterworks show like none other.

As we gathered up our gear, several thanked us for allowing them to be a part of the surprise. Once we got to the car, Kassi burst out, "Oh, Mom, I am so mad at you for making me cry in front of all those people." I laughed and said, "No you're not. You're too happy to be mad."

Most of the way home we rode in silence, a smile never leaving her face. Finally, she said, "Mom, that was good. That is the best surprise I've ever had." *John 17:18 says: "In the same way that you gave me a mission in the world, I gave them a mission in the world." (MSG).* I am in awe of how God perfectly planted the right question at the perfect time, even without my manipulating and controlling it. He had given us the final assurance that indeed, we were going back to Africa to love the beautiful children on His behalf.

Letting Go

The day I dreaded arrived. As we left the house, I watched our son Tucker walk through each room as if memorizing his childhood home. I watched him spend a sweet moment with each of the pets. I watched him pause and look around one final time. Then it was time to start the three-hour drive to take him to the Navy recruiting station. The quiet drive passed with a flood of emotion, each mile ticking away with a sense of loss and heaviness.

After a special dinner together, we went to our separate hotel rooms for the night, but my mind wouldn't stop thinking. Tucker must have been lying awake too, as he sent a text. "Mom, do you think I'm really ready?"

I texted back, "Of course you are love. You've prepared and planned for this for a long time." What I really wanted to write was, "No, let's go home NOW and forget this whole idea." But I knew Tucker's plan to launch into manhood included this dream. I prayed it would lead him to his God-given purpose.

We continued to text back and forth for hours as we shared memories and talked of the future adventure that awaited him. The next morning, we met him at the recruiting center to witness his swearing in. We proudly watched him commit to serve his country, and like the passing of a baton, he passed from our hands into that of the United States Navy. Then it was time to say goodbye, the first of many goodbyes. Our eyes were red from holding back tears. With a final kiss and hug, we watched him go. The dreaded moment had arrived, time to let him go.

On the way home, our youngest son Josh and I held hands in the backseat of the car as we let the tears fall. I kept thinking of the little boy who had grown up way too fast. I thought of how he'd never been on a flight alone and yet, now flying to make connections to Chicago. I thought of how lonely my evening walks were going to be without him, my beloved son, but also my friend.

In the days that passed, we missed Tucker so much. Every day, he was in our thoughts and prayers. As the recruiter advised, I wrote him letters trying to make life sound normal, even though nothing seemed normal. When letters came from him, sharing vulnerable feelings and concerns, again my mama's heart broke. Despite it all, he showed bravery, so I tried to do the same. *1 Peter 5:7* says: *"Cast all your anxieties on Him because he cares for you." (NIV)*

Although daily life seemed to fly by in a blur, it felt like he'd been gone for years even though it had only been weeks. The emptiness in our home seemed to grow, but Kassi and Joshua helped fill the void. Finally, the time came to celebrate his graduation from boot camp. I was never prouder to be a mother and an American. Our time went too fast, which meant another goodbye. It never got easier, but FaceTime made our separation bearable, being able to see his face and hear his voice.

In the years that followed, we missed Tucker at family weddings, at graduations, at birthdays, and at holidays. I missed him most during my evening walks when we used to talk about life, ideas, and future plans.

When we remember and honor the Veterans, I do so from the personal perspective of a mama who felt the grief of letting her son go. We missed out on years of his life as he served his country both state-side and during overseas deployments. In that season, our son became a man, willing to sacrifice his life for his country. I am so proud to be the mama of an American serviceman and now a Veteran.

God bless those who serve our country and the families who support them.

Happy Birthday Amy

August 23rd arrived, just like every other year. Twenty-four years ago today, we held our beautiful stillborn daughter Amy. As the years passed, my first thought of the day was of Amy's birthday followed by, "Today Amy would have been x years old." This year was no different.

Rolling out of bed, I felt a familiar sadness. We should have been celebrating a birthday, but instead, just like every other year, August 23rd would be a quiet day, privately thinking of our little girl who never celebrated a birthday.

For years my sister Colleen faithfully sent flowers. She never missed a year wishing Amy Colleen, her namesake, Happy Birthday. I loved it, but after eighteen years of her beautiful gift, I told her it wasn't necessary to continue. Reluctantly, she stopped sending flowers annually but still continued to text a short message remembering Amy.

With Amy on my mind, I prepared for church. I needed to get there early to help with several volunteer responsibilities. My friend Pam would be volunteering with me.

Arriving at church, Pam and I greeted one another and then she reached into her bag. "I have something for you," she said.

"For me?" I asked, uncertain why.

"Yes." Then she handed me a beautiful little square box with a pretty bow and added, "This is a Happy Birthday for you and Amy."

Tears quickly sprang to my eyes. Surprised, I asked, "How did you know?"

Pam explained, "Well, you know I've been reading your book, **Love To Give**. Last night I decided to put it down for the night, but then felt a nudge to read one more chapter. So I did. In that next chapter, I learned today was Amy's birthday. I felt like God wanted me to give this to you."

By now we were both crying as the men folk looked on with wonder. They never quite understand how we ladies can erupt into tears so quickly. I opened the box and inside lay a beautiful silver bracelet with a heart shaped clasp. Attached were two charms, one that read "Love" and the other that read "Daughter".

Yes, there were more tears and hugs. After another thank you, I put the bracelet on my wrist and headed into worship. I don't think I took my eyes off the bracelet the entire time. Such a surprise. I am in awe of how God blessed me in a way that made the day not seem quite so sad.

So, once again, Happy Birthday Amy. I've never stopped missing you darling.

Africa Bound Again?

After two trips to Africa, it seemed inconceivable the team from our church would go back without us. On faith, Kassi and I committed to go for a third time, having no idea how we'd come up with the resources to get there. The price had now grown to $3,200 per person, with half due in a week.

As Kassi and I were driving home from school, I finally said what needed to be said, "Honey, I don't think we'll be able to go to Africa this year. We're $1,300 away from the first half that must be turned in next week." We both started to cry, neither of us wanting to miss being part of the mission team. With desperation in her voice, Kassi implored me to trust God. "Honey, I do, but I also have to be realistic. I'm out of ideas on how to come up with the rest of the funds to pay for the first half, let alone the final half that will be due in a couple of months." Quiet filled the car as we both processed our disappointment.

When I got home, I prayed again and then I thought of Kassi's school costs. In the fall, we'd enrolled her in a private high school and had paid for the whole year up-front. After the first semester, Kassi decided she would rather be with her friends in public school. Being away from them at the same time her brother had left for the Navy proved to be too lonely. So, we moved her back to the public school for the second semester. At that time, I had asked for a refund but hadn't felt I'd been fairly reimbursed. As a last-ditch effort, I wrote a letter to the school and asked them to re-evaluate the amount of my refund.

The following week, I received a call from the school. The lady apologized and then told me that indeed, they made a mistake on the amount that should have been refunded. She told me she was authorizing a check to me in the amount of $1,317, almost exactly what we needed to make the first half of the payment for the trip. I could hardly believe it!

I couldn't wait to tell Kassi. With new energy, we went to work raising money for the second half. We sold cookie dough, had a garage sale, and scrimped and saved. When the second half came due, we had the money raised! Our third trip to Africa turned out to be our final trip, but what a lesson we learned in how God provides when our hearts are set on His purpose and plans.

Psalm 37:23 "The steps of a man are established by the Lord, when he delights in his way." (ESV)

Awe God

Seating Assignment

As I slid into my seat, I greeted the young couple sitting next to me on the plane. I soon learned they were from Ethiopia. He was sixteen and she, his older sister. As we started to taxi out of the airport and onto the runway, I learned this young man, sandwiched between myself and his sister, was terrified of flying. Not only that, but he was legally blind, and we were on a transoceanic flight from the United States to Africa!

Now all that might not seem like a big deal until one realizes seventeen hours sitting next to a terrified young man is indeed a long time, especially when the typical distractions don't work because, did I mention, he was legally blind? Even so, the hours crept by and my own fatigue became apparent. In an effort to distract him, I'd suggest watching a movie or reading a book, only to realize my stupidity since, yes, he was legally blind.

So it went, hour after hour. I'm not going to lie; he gave me a workout. Every jiggle or bump during our ride, just as I finally nodded off to sleep, he'd grab my hand. Sometimes he cried out "Mama". Glancing at his sister, she returned a weary look of exhaustion. She had long ago given up trying to comfort him, so I simply held his hand and tried to remind him there was nothing to fear.

I thought of my own sons who were teens themselves. I missed them so much. Tucker had left our home and now served for our country in the Navy. Josh, although still at home, felt so far away as I traveled across the globe to Ethiopia. My mama's heart ached for my sons as I acknowledged in their growing up, they didn't need me as much. I missed them deeply. Sitting next to this young man,

I felt needed as a mama again. I also couldn't help but think about how I'd want a stranger to treat my boys if they were on a plane under these circumstances.

By the time we reached Africa, I probably looked like a drunk as I staggered off the plane from pure exhaustion. As we departed, the young siblings hugged me and thanked me profusely. I thanked them both, and then reminded the young man what bravery it took to make that long flight. For extra measure, I reminded them God is always with them, something seventeen hours together had given us ample time to discuss.

Although I expected to travel to Africa to then begin my mission, God gave me an assignment while we were still in flight. In addition, God gave me assurances I was still mama to my boys, even if their independence made it feel like I wasn't needed as much. I am quite certain God put that young man next to me, not because I am such a great seatmate, but simply because I am a mom. That young boy needed a mama as much as this mama needed a boy to comfort. Sometimes the mission field is as simple as that.

"And our hope for you is firm, because we know that just as you share in our sufferings, so also you share in our comfort." 2 Corinthians 1:7 (NIV) Our Heavenly Father really does have this comfort thing down.

Something's Missing

As I stepped off the bus, a crowd of people surged forward. A woman stretched her hand out to me. Somehow, I suppressed a gasp. She had no fingers! Her outstretched hand was only a palm. Leprosy had eaten away her digits. I realized her empty palm wouldn't be able to even grasp what might be placed there. Without fingers, she wouldn't be able to do simple tasks, like buttoning her blouse. I couldn't imagine how hard life must be for her.

In Ethiopia, such sights were all around us. People with missing limbs making their way on makeshift crutches. Women stooped over due to carrying heavy loads on their heads, yet still carrying jugs of water. A man without legs scooting around on his behind, his calloused fists like clubs as they served as his feet. Yet, they were all somehow making it, maybe not thriving, but surviving.

As I've been on this journey of life, I've often reflected on the fingerless lady. I realized I'm a lot like her. Perhaps not physically, but so often I am missing something important to carry out a task. Like when God first prompted me to be a foster parent, but I lacked the courage to give up another baby and yet, we did. Or when I realized my calling to advocate for children and families in foster care would require testifying at legislative committees, even though it made me weak in the knees at the very thought. Or in helping my mother die, navigating medications and her comfort while also struggling with my own emotions of her loss. Even that trip to Ethiopia, observing so many people with disabilities, caused this Montana girl to get way outside of my comfort zone and do what I'd never thought I could.

God often asks us to do something beyond our abilities, skills, or mental capacity. He even asks us to do so when we aren't ready or prepared. Yet, He has shown over and over it isn't about what we bring, but rather what He brings. In fact, we're probably more effective in our voids because it keeps us humble, leaning, and dependent on God. Our only role is to be willing and available; to stand up, speak up, reach out, and present whatever we have to offer for the Lord to use as He wills, even if it feels like it's just fingerless hands.

Colossians 3:23-24 "Whatever you do, work heartily, as for the Lord and not for men, knowing that from the Lord you will receive the inheritance as your reward. You are serving the Lord Christ." (ESV).

Making Room

Our oldest son Tucker was getting married. As we arrived in California, the excitement of being with him and his fiancé couldn't be contained. We'd rented a home where we would all be staying. I knew they would be waiting there for us.

Although the flight arrived on time, the checkout line for the rental car stretched for what felt like miles. When we finally arrived at the car rental counter, a polite man told us our mid-sized car wasn't ready! I could have cried. He paused to look at his computer and then added, "However, there is a van ready now if you'd rather have that."

"Ready now!" That's all we needed to hear so with van keys in hand, we loaded into our van and within minutes, were on the road. An hour later, we pulled into the driveway of the home. Tucker and Mica were waiting up, but our soon to be granddaughter, three-year-old Leena, had fallen asleep. Kisses would have to wait until morning.

With a few days left before the wedding, there were some last-minute errands to run. We shopped for groceries and filled the back of the van with food. Then we picked up wedding supplies, tuxes, and decorations and again, filled the van. The day of the wedding arrived and once again we filled the van, this time with the wedding dress, decorations, and everything else that would fit.

The wedding ceremony overflowed with joy, a gorgeous, fun, memorable, and blessed event. Oh, how I loved adding two beautiful young ladies to our family. Exhausted at the end of the night, again we stuffed the van with gifts, left-over cake, decorations, and most importantly, a very tired little Leena. As our daughter Kassi buckled Leena into her car seat, one of the only places still left to sit, Leena gave a tired sigh and said, "It's time to go home. Now we're a family." Oh, from the mouths of babes. Her sweet comment defined what the day was about: enlarging our family and making room for more.

The next morning, the extended family joined us at the rental house to watch the newlywed's open gifts. The day passed too quickly, and the next day, we loaded the van, filling every vacant space with gifts and food to drop off at Tucker & Mica's apartment. With final hugs, we headed back to the airport.

As our week of celebration came to an end, we dropped our van off at the airport. Handing the keys back at the car rental counter, I felt immense gratitude. God, in His usual way, filled our need long before we even knew it was necessary, ensuring we had a van for the many occasions when we needed more room.

I shouldn't have been surprised. After all, He is a God who always makes room. When Christ was born, He made room in a stable. A relationship with Christ is simply making room in our hearts for Him to be the Lord of our lives. Upon Jesus' departure from earth, He promised that *"My Father's house has many rooms...I am going there to prepare a place for you." John 14:2 (NIV)* Can you imagine what that room will be like?

Of course, it was just a van, but God used it as a powerful reminder of how He's made room for us. I pray every day I will make room for Him to work through my life, for His glory.

Time Out

Someone needed a time out and that someone was me! I needed a break and there seemed no better place than going to see my mom.

It had been a particularly challenging season of pushing through some really tough stuff as well as ongoing demands. I had run out of steam. I hadn't gotten out of the house much except to work and run errands. I couldn't remember when I'd even taken time for a walk with my neighbor. My favorite swing on the back porch remained vacant and still all summer. I hadn't even spent regular time reading my Bible, leaving me dried up and tired.

Making the three-hour drive to Helena, I listened to Christian music while letting the tears fall. It would be nice to sleep in, and not have to do anything or be available for anyone for a few days. When I arrived at Mom's, we visited, caught up on the happenings in Helena, admired her sewing projects, took some walks, and shared thoughts and concerns. As the weekend came to an end, Mom shed some tears as we said our goodbyes. She told me how much she appreciated me sharing time and conversation with her.

As I drove home, I reflected on Mom's words, how much she appreciated me "sharing time and conversation" with her. It caused me to think of one of the reasons why I needed my "time out".

Our young adult son faced a crossroads in his life, making major decisions that would be life altering. He hadn't shared much nor asked for our input. It made me sad, because sharing is one of the things we always did so well. Now, wounded and hurting, he attempted to navigate unknown territory on his own. I just wish he would talk things out with us.

Denise E. Johnson

As parents, we understand more than our children sometimes give us credit for. We've made mistakes too, but with experiences and lessons learned, we can help the next generation. Talking about major decisions helps prepare everyone for what comes next.

My thoughts turned to my own weariness, a result of this hard season in life. I had to admit, some of this burden I felt was because I too had been trying to carry the weight myself, not sharing with my heavenly Father. Sure, I had prayed. In fact, I'd prayed more in this past year than any other season of my life, but my prayers had been more about my pains and worries than my gratitude. They were one-sided, not pausing to listen to what God might have to say. I wondered if He too felt left out, observing me make decisions and choices without His input.

Jesus' words in Matthew 11:28 came to mind: *"Come to me, all of you who are weary and burdened, and I will give you rest." (NIV)*. Like going home to visit Mom, and like me wishing my son would come talk with me, Jesus wants us to come to Him and lay our concerns and burdens at His feet.

Hebrews 4:14-16: Now that we know what we have—Jesus, this great High Priest with ready access to God—let's not let it slip through our fingers. We don't have a priest who is out of touch with our reality. He's been through weakness and testing, experienced it all—all but the sin. So let's walk right up to him and get what he is so ready to give. Take the mercy, accept the help. (MSG).

Unexpected Flight

I love to be spontaneous, particularly if it means I get to travel. It's even better when it's God's idea!

I had no plans for the day except to get over this nasty cold. When my daughter-in-law sent me a text message, I sensed concern in her voice. Her most recent calls indicated she was seeking advice, maybe even seeking God. I texted a response, "At the risk of sounding like a broken record, only Jesus can heal brokenness. I would love to see you find a church or ladies Bible study group."

Immediately I felt a prompting of the Lord, encouraging me to help her find one. Since she lived in the Seattle area, miles from me, that meant doing a Google search. I scurried to my computer and began my search. A page of options popped up. I randomly clicked on a website and checked for studies. Sure enough, a lady's group was starting in two weeks, a Lysa Terkeurst study called "It Wasn't Supposed to Be This Way." Wow, what a perfect study. I had always wanted to do one of Lysa's studies. I felt envious that I couldn't be a part of it.

I messaged my daughter-in-law and told her it would be a great study with only a six-week commitment, a nice length for the first study. Before hitting send, I attached the link. Then I waited. No response.

God reminded me of how nervous I had been so many years ago to go to my first Bible study. A friend ultimately invited me and I appreciated having someone to go with me. By now, my mind whirled with an idea: Why not go with her to her first one? Plus, it would give me an excuse to do one of Lysa's studies, even if I had to finish it remotely.

I checked my calendar and realized the study began during a brief break in my schedule, so I began searching for flights. Finally, I checked out my mileage program and realized I had just enough miles to cover my roundtrip ticket. My heart pounded as I realized this could actually happen.

Off went another message to my daughter-in-law. "How about if I fly out to join you? It would give me an excuse to spoil my granddaughter and spend a few days with you."

No message followed. Then a minute later the phone rang. "Are you crazy?" she asked. I chuckled. Perhaps the time had come to admit what most of my family already surmised! Yep, I was crazy. Then she added rather timidly, "We always love having family come visit."

My heart skipped a beat. "So, that's a yes?" No response. Perhaps she thought I was kidding. I continued to pursue my idea: "How close do you live to the church listed in the flier?"

"It's only a few miles from our house!" Goosebumps ran down my arms. In the entire Seattle area, the church that happened to have a Bible study at the first site I'd googled, that would start at the exact time I could sneak away, and fly with my free ticket, just happened to be in their neighborhood. It was providential. What a big and wonderful God to arrange such amazing details. Before the call ended, I booked the flight.

Isaiah 6:8 says, "And I heard the voice of the Lord saying, 'Whom shall I send, and who will go for us?' Then I said, 'Here I am! Send me." (ESV)

Maybe a trip out to join my daughter-in-law at Bible study with the bonus of seeing my granddaughter and son doesn't count as being "sent", but two weeks later, that's exactly what I did.

There is no doubt that our God is on the move. I'm so glad He lets me fly with Him.

Going to Jail

My sweet young friend Sarah had called. She sobbed into the phone as she told me a series of poor choices and wrong accusations had landed her in jail. She begged me to visit so I promised I would.

The next day I called to learn about visiting hours. They were on Wednesday, two days away. I put the time in my calendar so I wouldn't miss the opportunity to go and encourage her.

Wednesday came with its usual fill of responsibilities. A conversation delayed me from leaving on time, so I arrived forty-five minutes late. I hoped I'd still get to see her.

I locked my car and crossed the parking lot. People were streaming out and disappointment filled me. Perhaps I was too late. I picked up my pace and as I entered, I noticed a large waiting area, full of people. Another group of people formed a long line passing through a door to the back. I looked around seeking direction on what to do. Behind the line of people, I noticed a desk with a sign, "Visitors must sign in," along with another sign, "Once you've signed in, do not leave the waiting area". As the last of the visitors cleared the area, I made my way to the desk and caught the attention of the attendant.

Before I could even speak, the attendant looked away and put her finger to her earpiece, listening. Then she called out, "Anyone here for Sarah?" I raised my hand. She nodded to acknowledge me.

"I haven't signed in yet," I confessed as I fished out my identification. She pointed to the tablet on the table and without giving me another look, turned toward the waiting area and repeated, "Anyone here for Sarah?"

When no one stepped forward, she turned back to me, "You can take that visit then since no one else is here." With that, she opened the large door and motioned me through.

Sarah sat behind the heavy glass window as she waited for her visitor. Tears were in her eyes. Her hands were cuffed as she sat shaking in her chair. We talked for twenty minutes and, when our time neared the end, I prayed for her. As we parted, Sarah had a smile on her face.

When I re-entered the waiting area, I felt puzzled about how I managed to visit without having signed in. I stopped to ask the attendant about typical protocol so I would know what to do in the future.

"Normally visitation starts at 3:00. Today it was delayed. Once you sign in, we'll call the prisoner forward for the visit."

I thanked her and left the building. As I walked to my car, I felt an overwhelming sense of awe at what God had just done. Although I had arrived later than planned, I was there at the exact time to see Sarah. Although I hadn't signed in, God had reserved a spot for me. Talk about a prison miracle. Perhaps not like Peter being taken out of prison by an angel, or Paul's prison doors being opened by an earthquake, but God's hand certainly guided on our visit. What a great reminder for Sarah that He never forgets us no matter where we are.

Deuteronomy 31:6 "Be strong and courageous. Do not be afraid or terrified because of them, for the LORD your God goes with you; he will never leave you nor forsake you." (NIV)

Life's a Mess

In our life's journey, people can be a tremendous help or they can be a hindrance. Let's face it, people are messy. We do and say brilliant things AND we do and say stupid things. No one is exempt, but we can all choose what to do with the messes of life. One of the most important things we can do is to show compassion and grace toward others, even if we don't agree or perhaps even like each other.

I'd like to challenge us to do five things:

1) Look at our most recent social media posts. Were they encouraging? Did they lift people up? Did they make the world better or safer? Or did they spew judgment or divisiveness?

2) Think about the words we've said. Were they words we'd like someone to say about or to our child? Or are they words that would bring out the Mama or Papa bear in us?

3) Is there grace in our countenance or do we carry around smug smiles of self-righteousness and hatred, complete with a pointed finger of accusation?

4) Are we acknowledging that all human lives matter, even if they aren't our flesh and blood? Even if we don't agree with them? Or are we behaving like the only people that matter are the ones we agree with or call our family?

5) Do our words honor people as God's children? Do they reflect a heart for humanity or a cruelty and intolerance for others?

Do I get it right all the time? Absolutely not. You see, I'm one of those messy people who does messy things. I've hurt others when I didn't communicate well and allowed offenses to create walls. I've also lived out painful messes caused by others.

Messes are a part of life which means we all have work to do. We have people to hug, children to rescue, and issues to pray for. To accomplish the hard work that needs to be done, we have to roll up our sleeves and get right in the middle of the mess. To do anything less is a waste of our energy and our God-given gift of time. Let's commit to showing love, grace, and understanding. Let's decide there is no room in our lives for hatred, contempt, or disrespect toward ANYONE. Let's go bless others with the lessons from our own messes.

Philippians 4:8-9: "Finally, brothers, whatever is true, whatever is honorable, whatever is just, whatever is pure, whatever is lovely, whatever is commendable, if there is any excellence, if there is anything worthy of praise, think about these things. What you have learned and received and heard and seen in me—practice these things, and the God of peace will be with you." (ESV)

Ephesians 2:14: "For he himself is our peace, who has made us both one and has broken down in his flesh the dividing wall of hostility." (ESV)

New Hope

Reading through his story, I found it hard to even fathom. The desperation this little guy must have felt was beyond anything I could imagine. His life had been about rejection, neglect, loneliness, and hunger. As one of millions of orphans in Ethiopia, he had been fortunate to be noticed and rescued from the streets. He now lived at an orphanage called New Hope Center.

 Six years ago, my daughter Kassi and I made a trip to Africa to be a part of a mission team to New Hope. Being part of the team changed our lives, and when the trip concluded, we knew we had to go back. The next two years, we were able to return and with each trip, the children became dearer to us. Due to a number of personal issues, we hadn't been back for three years. My heart ached for the darlings we loved so much. They were growing up without us.

 To continue being part of them, I had taken on the role of helping to match sponsors with children, assisting on-site staff who identified and brought new children into the orphanage. In this role, I had the privilege of reading each of the children's stories. Each story told of tragedy and loss. Many of the children were AIDS orphans. Others had disabilities or were abandoned by their parents. All came from horrible living conditions and had no access to basic food and shelter, let alone an education.

 When our church first heard of this little orphanage almost twelve years ago, the government was threatening to shut it down. Without adequate financial support, the children were starving just as they had on the streets. Upon hearing the plight of New Hope, our church stepped in. Now the orphanage was on solid ground and the children were growing and healthy. Not only were the children growing, the number of children served had grown. This past year, eight more children had been rescued, bringing the total to sixty-six children, almost double the number from our last trip.

To meet the needs of the children, we needed three sponsors for each child. We had an annual sponsorship weekend at church with the intention of getting every child fully sponsored. As the sponsorship weekend wrapped up, we were still four sponsors short. Then I learned one of the current sponsors had unintentionally overpaid, so he asked to apply his funds to two more children. Then, due to the connection of the doctor who worked closely with the children, another woman stepped forward, but that still left one child in need of an additional sponsor.

After working for several hours on the sponsorship paperwork, I left the church, thinking of that one child who needed one more sponsor. When I reached my car, I realized I had forgotten my notebook, so I turned around and returned to the church. As I entered, a friend saw me and waved me over to her table. She introduced me to her friend and after a brief conversation, I learned this friend wanted to sponsor a child. I could hardly respond, so stunned.

Had I not walked back into the church at that moment, I would have gone home thinking of that one child, but God wasn't going to settle for anything less than needed. Once again, I was reminded of God's provision. He knew before those sweet children were even brought into the orphanage; they would need sponsors. He filled every single need, just like He always does.

"Commit your way to the Lord; trust in him, and he will act." Psalm 37:5 (ESV)

What a Bag!

Suffice it to say that everything was coming down around me. The nagging pain reminded me of my inflamed rotator cuff. We'd just learned our son had a concerning genetic issue. To top it off, our daughter was in crisis, causing tremendous stress in the family. It all culminated in tension at home as Ron and I struggled to handle it without becoming the "crazy family".

Although physically and emotionally hurting, the spiritual aspect trumped it all. Like never before, I felt the attack of the enemy in heightened levels. There had been past seasons of grief, loss, and tragedy, but this time it felt like all-out war for souls and lives. A battle raged, making it feel as if pain would take up permanent residence with consequences that would have lifelong impacts.

Thank goodness I have my faith, knowing God is bigger than all my challenges combined. He is with me and thus, I'm not alone. He will not waste any pain, but will use it for my good and His glory. I know my good God will never allow things to happen in my life without first passing through His hands. Still, I felt weary.

Life goes on though, right? Amid so many heavy and hard things, you still have to pay the bills, do the laundry, and clean the house. Beyond that, I'd offered to host a Bridal Shower for a friend months ago. With it only four days away, I needed to get my plans together. I went to the computer searching for bridal shower games. By noon, I had the games figured out. In past weeks, I managed to purchase decorations and paper supplies along with three door prize bags. With the games now planned, I realized I'd need another prize bag. With my list in hand, I headed to get one additional bag plus a few other supplies.

Arriving at the store, I went directly to the gift bag area where I had previously purchased the decorations. My heart sank as I realized those specific bags were gone. There were larger ones and smaller ones, but not the size I needed. I stood there staring at the bag section for the longest time, as if it would somehow magically show up on the rack. Finally, after over-thinking the issue several different ways, I decided to repackage all four door prizes. It wouldn't work to have three bags that matched and one that didn't. I put four new bags in my cart and proceeded to take care of the rest of my list.

After picking up a gift from the bridal registry, I realized I needed wrapping paper and remembered seeing paper that matched the bags. (Yes, it had to match). So, I headed back to the gift bag aisle, but entered from the opposite end. As I turned into the aisle, I stopped in my tracks. Right there, completely out of place, hanging at an awkward angle was one lone bag that matched the three I'd already purchased. Tears welled up in my eyes as I whispered to myself, "Look how much God loves me."

During a very heavy, very exhausting, very trying season, God had shown me He cared about even the most minute detail of my life. It was just a stupid gift bag, but it reminded me that if God ensured I had that one gift bag, He surely would be working on the harder stuff too.

Psalm 46:10 "Be Still and Know That I Am God." (ESV). Oh yes He is, and I have a bag to prove it!

Thy Will Be Done

My god-brother Scott had a ticket to fly to San Diego at 1:30 pm. We still didn't have the necessary paperwork to make it happen, which caused a fitful night. I worried we wouldn't be able to obtain it in time.

Early in the morning, we got up to drive to the office where we hoped we could obtain the last document. We wanted to be there when the doors opened at 7:00 am.

As we made our trip across town, we both expressed our concerns. "Let's pray about it," I said to Scott. Since I was driving, I kept my eyes straight ahead. Lowering the volume on the radio so we could focus on our prayer, I reached to grab Scott's hand and we prayed. As we wrapped up, my eyes strayed to the dashboard. The radio lit up the word "Scott". I stared as the next words, "Thy Will Be Done", scrolled across the display. Excitedly I said to Scott, "Did you see that?"

"Yes," he choked out. "What a reminder this is all about God's will."

We cranked up the volume on KLOVE and sang along to Hilary Scott's song, Thy Will be Done, that just happened to be playing at that exact moment. It was as if God had written a private message to Scott, to both of us, on my dashboard. He reminded us even in our worry wrought with tight timelines, God's will would be done.

So it was. We obtained the necessary documents and drove the two hours to Bozeman to catch his flight. As I watched Scott make his way through security, paperwork in hand, I couldn't help but reflect on how distinctly God reminded us, when it comes to the plans and purpose of the Lord, His will would be done!

"The Lord works out everything to its proper end..." Proverbs 16:4 (NIV)

The Quilt

Have you ever heard the saying, there are two kinds of people? The first are people who come into the room and announce, "I'm here", thus drawing attention to themselves. The second are people who walk into a room, survey it, and when they see others say, "You're here", making others feel special and recognized.

My friend Roxi is one of those in the second category. When we first met, we became instant friends. She has a way of making one feel like they are her best friend, even though she has oodles of friends. In hindsight, I know why God gave us such an instant draw of friendship, but I'll get to that in a second.

Within months of meeting Roxi, she learned she had a major health challenge. Then the unthinkable happened; her infant granddaughter, Naomi, was placed in foster care. Her birth had been very traumatic which caused head trauma. Only months old, she needed medical attention, and when her parents took her to the hospital, they were accused of child abuse. It was unthinkable; they were loving devoted parents who would never harm their child.

Compounding my shock for what happened to Naomi and her parents was concern for Roxi. What a tremendous burden for her to carry while dealing with her own health issues. In the worst way, I wanted to see Roxi and support her. I called her to see if we could make a visit happen, but it looked like it would have to wait until spring.

Since I'd been making children's rag quilts, I decided to make one for Naomi, expectant that she would be coming home soon. We would trust God for that outcome. Since I wouldn't be able to see Roxi until the spring and sister Colleen had ordered five quilts for Christmas, I didn't give Naomi's quilt any thought.

One fall morning, I woke with a strange sense of urgency to start Naomi's quilt. It seemed irrational, but I couldn't seem to shake it, so off I went to the fabric store. I fell in love with a combination of yellow and orange fabric. I promptly went home and cut out the quilt, finishing it up by the end of the weekend.

The following week I called Roxi. I could hear her sadness over the phone and knew I couldn't wait until spring. I needed to encourage and support her somehow. Upon checking flights to Denver, I noticed discounted tickets for the upcoming weekend. I called Roxi, "What would you say if I came down this weekend?" She loved the idea.

That weekend, I arrived in Denver and we shared a much-needed hug. We talked for hours, played card games, and prayed together. When I gave Roxi Naomi's quilt, she cried, commenting that the colors matched Naomi's nursery. When we parted, after our fast weekend, I felt blessed to have shared some time together.

God used Naomi's case to prompt me to research the foster care crisis in the United States. That launched me into a new ministry, advocating for families involved with child protection services. He had been orchestrating it all, building on the various experiences of my life, preparing me for my next ministry, right down to making sure the baby quilt was done on time.

"But I do not account my life of any value nor as precious to myself, if only I may finish my course and the ministry that I received from the Lord Jesus, to testify to the gospel of the grace of God." Acts 20:24 (ESV). God has a plan for all of us, a purpose and ministry. If you don't know what yours is yet, look at what God has put in your life. Perhaps there are common threads he's maturing. Stay close to God and if you feel a nudge, go with it! He will make His plan clear, giving us the opportunity to partake in testifying of the grace of God.

Naomi's story is in the Epilogue of my first book, **Love To Give**. My second book, **For The Children** was inspired in part by their journey through the foster care system.

Christmas Blessings

Every Christmas I try to think of a unique way to do something special for someone who might not be on my normal shopping list. In past years, we've bought chickens for the underprivileged, sponsored children in Africa, and bought clothes for needy children. We've served meals at the mission, invited friends to join us who might otherwise spend the holidays alone, and bought presents for children on the Angel Tree.

One year I learned a coworker was struggling to make ends meet due to a medical crisis. So, the kids and I hit the grocery store and loaded up a cart. Then under the cover of darkness, we drove to her neighborhood, parked the car a few houses away, carried the groceries to her doorstep, and then "ding-dong-ditched" her. We giggled as we tripped over the snow and each other, trying to make haste to our car before she got to the door. Then we sat in the car, trying to stifle our laughter as we watched her open her door and look around.

Another year I gave each of our children $40 and told them to spend it on someone who needed it more than they did. Kassi gave it to her coach who recently received a cancer diagnosis. Our youngest son Josh put it in the Salvation Army bucket. Tucker bought new shoes for a classmate who really needed them. Afterwards he said to me, "Mom, why haven't we done that every year? That was the best gift I've ever given."

This year I heard of an idea where people would get in line at the grocery store behind someone who looks like they could use a hand and then step forward to pay for their groceries. What a fun idea, but I hadn't put my plan into action yet. In fact, I hadn't really given it much thought since hearing about it because, like most of us during the holiday season, I was BUSY! So, God took matters into His own hands and gave me a nudge as He often does when I'm not paying attention to His direction.

I learned an acquaintance needed a ride to an appointment, so I offered to take her. On the way home, she mentioned she needed a few groceries, so I suggested we stop at the grocery store before delivering her back home. At the store, she modestly filled her cart. God reminded me of the Christmas idea and knowing her budget was limited, I asked, "Is there something that isn't in your budget that you'd enjoy for Christmas?" After assuring her I wanted to get it for her, she added a few more items. Then when we went through the checkout counter, I purchased everything in her cart, just as God had instructed. Her gratitude and joy made my day.

I don't share this to toot my own horn, but rather to share a lesson I learned: In the midst of crazy, chaotic seasons that often revolve around holidays, if we leave some margins in our schedule, God will use us in ways we might not anticipate. In the process, we are blessed in ways we would never imagine.

2 Corinthians 9:7, "Each one must give as he has decided in his heart, not reluctantly or under compulsion, for God loves a cheerful giver." (ESV). Our time, energy, talents, and resources are His, so give generously that which belongs to Him.

A New Thing

New Years is one of my favorite times of the year. Maybe it's because New Year's Eve brings fond memories of when my husband proposed, but I think it's more than that. With a new year, there is a fresh sense of promise. It's as if we get to hit a reset button. The past year, good, bad, or ugly is officially over. The new year is full of hope, optimism, and wonder.

Since our first year of marriage, I've kept a journal, recording the significant events of the past year and writing out our New Year's resolutions. As I wrote out the goals for the new year, instead of a list of what I planned to do, I wrote a list of what I wasn't going to do. I felt God nudging me to let go of my volunteer activities. Initially I questioned it. Why would God want me to give up things that were such good causes?

The more I questioned it, the more convicted I felt. So, I resigned from my volunteer activities and almost immediately, felt a sense of relief. Then came new opportunities I could have never imagined. My biggest cheerleader, sister Colleen, gifted me the opportunity to go to a Christian Writers Conference in California. I couldn't wait to go and learn more about writing.

Then, out of the blue, a job offer came for a position with a non-profit that provides services to children in foster care, where my true passion lies. I would not have even considered these opportunities if I were still up to my eyeballs in my volunteer work. It seemed like a message from God: "You have to let something go, so I can give you the work I really need you to do!"

Isaiah 43:19 reminds us that there are seasons of change. *"See, I am doing a new thing! Now it springs up; do you not perceive it? I am making a way in the wilderness and streams in the wasteland." (NIV)*

Yes Lord, I'm finally perceiving it! If God is making a way through this wilderness of life, then I want to be right on His heels. I'm so grateful we serve such a patient God, who makes a way for opportunities and blesses us with new ways to serve His purposes!

Awe God

To-Do List

Colleen, my brother Dave and I had been planning an 80th birthday party for Mom and invited over 100 guests. We had gone all out for her special day as we organized entertainment, put together a picture video, planned around a Cat in the Hat theme, and ordered refreshments with an amazing sewing machine shaped cake. We were so excited to celebrate with Mom.

Two days before we were to drive to Helena, Ron ended up in the emergency room with chest pains. The doctors couldn't identify what caused them, so they wanted him to remain in the hospital over the weekend, and planned to do a heart catheter on Monday. Ron encouraged us to go to Helena without him. The crisis had passed and there really wasn't anything we could do. Still, I felt torn. What kind of a wife leaves her husband in the cardiac unit alone? He reminded us he was in capable hands at the hospital, thus no need to worry, and so we left, making our way to celebrate Mom's birthday.

Mom loved every moment of her party and we all left with fun memories of our weekend celebrating her. Back home, Ron's heart catheter showed minor blockages, but nothing urgent. After five days in the hospital, he came home with new medication and a changed perspective on the value of life. Adjustments needed to be made in our overflowing life schedules.

Slowing down our schedule would need to wait though, since the following weekend, I would fly to California for the Christian Writers Conference. Although beyond excited to go, I questioned leaving Ron. Again, he encouraged me to go, assuring me all would be fine.

With so much happening in the past week, I wasn't as prepared for my trip as I wanted. Part of the experience allowed me to submit an unpublished manuscript to agents who would critique it. Colleen had been encouraging me to write a fictional story, so I had a few chapters done. Burning the midnight oil, I attempted to fine-tune them.

When morning came, I got up early, anxious to get back to work on my manuscript. As I headed down the stairs, I felt a tug to sit quietly with the Lord, but I was running out of time. I needed to keep moving so I'd be ready to board my plane. Surely, God would understand if I had to miss time together this morning. Yet, I couldn't shake it. My heart actually felt an aching to go sit with God.

Settling into my quiet place with my Bible in hand, I opened it to my bookmark and began reading *Ecclesiastes 12*. When I read verse 11, astonishment came over me. *"There's no end to the publishing of books, and constant study wears you out so you're no good for anything else." (MSG)*. I'm not kidding, that's what it said! Look it up yourself if you don't believe me!

I couldn't decide if I should laugh or cry. I mean seriously, could there have been a more appropriate scripture to read that day? To think some people actually think the Bible isn't relevant in today's world!

So, I shortened my to-do list and focused on time with Him. He had something to tell me and if I hadn't taken the time to be with Him, I would have missed His Message. Additionally, I might have been too worn out to even enjoy the conference I had been so looking forward to.

Is there something God has been trying to tell you that you've been too busy to hear? Are you too worn out that you're not good for anything else? Take a deep breath and go get your Bible. He's waiting for you!

Stretch Marks

None of us like them, right? Red streaks that remind us of how large we've become. Yet, often those stretch marks are a result of something amazing happening, like carrying a baby for nine months, or gaining muscle mass (or fat) rapidly! Regardless of what caused them, most of us don't want them.

Have you ever stopped to think we might be getting mental stretch marks too? Like when you learn of an unexpected pregnancy, or receive news of cancer, or have to accept a relationship is over. Changes in life cause us to mentally grow in ways we might never imagine or want.

The idea of mental stretch marks came to mind after taking a job with an organization I was passionate about. Right away, I felt stretched when asked to fill a position I hadn't been trained for. Since God had thrown open the door to this opportunity, I knew I needed to step through and trust Him. Soon, I realized the job itself wasn't going to be my biggest challenge. Instead, it would be the negative, hostile co-worker who made it very clear she didn't want me there.

As I tried to learn a new job, learn the names of dozens of co-workers, and the millions of tasks that come with a new job, I also tried to be Jesus to this co-worker, and she wasn't making it easy. I had many conversations with God as He reminded me that He loved her too, and thus I needed to be kind no matter how she treated me!

As the days stretched into weeks and months, I lobbed questions at God. Why did you put me in this hostile situation? Why does it have to be so hard? I could really, really love it here if it weren't for this co-worker. God remained quiet, and I knew I needed to continue letting those stretch marks widen and grow.

After some changes in the organization, I heard God say, "Stay until..." (the "until" is between God and me). About a month later, "until" happened. As clearly as I knew God had given me the job, I knew it was time to leave.

As I often do when I'm not ready to move or make a change, I tried to compromise with God. I spent the weekend praying about it and thinking about how I could delay my departure, because I really liked my job. I wanted to stay. Then I heard His still small voice say, "I never intended for you to stay long." Suddenly it occurred to me He had used my antagonistic co-worker to keep me from planting roots.

Still, I tried to reason with God. Surely, I could stay long enough to help train someone else to take over my job. Every day I stayed, more strain came, and it felt as if God said, "I said NOW!" It sounded a lot like what we parents say to our children when we're done discussing it's time to clean their room. I gave my notice and left, armed with new mental stretch marks, proof I'm growing in my walk with the Lord.

Soon after, the company folded and rumors circulated of its demise. God spared me the drama by directing me to leave when I did. Looking back, I realized God used that experience to give me knowledge, connections, and resources for the next phase of my life. After leaving the job, armed with new knowledge, I took the time to write and publish "**For The Children**". I began speaking to service organizations about the foster care crisis in our country. These opportunities led to an invitation to join a non-profit that supported families in crisis, which then catapulted me into working with the legislature on laws that better serve children in crisis.

God has a plan for all of our lives. He knows what seasons we need to be in, when we need to be there, what we need to learn in the process, and when we need to leave. Our job is simply to hear His voice and if necessary, stretch so we can be used according to His purposes. *Ecclesiastes 3:1 "For everything there is a season, and a time for every matter under heaven." (ESV)*

Misunderstood

It's happened to all of us. Something gets said (or not said) that is misunderstood. A reaction that wasn't expected, a word that came out wrong. Life is full of misunderstandings. Then if you add a dose of family drama, well now you've got something really explosive. If that's not enough, there's politics and religion. Now we have the makings of all-out-war. It's no longer a simple misunderstanding, but rather a battle that will leave someone wounded, injured, or rejected.

Ron and I went through a couple years of such misunderstanding, which resulted in close family members not even talking to each other. Sadly, the misunderstanding could have been resolved with a little compassion and understanding. Have you ever noticed when someone is right, there's no talking them out of it? Yep, when you're THAT right, it's pretty hard to see you're NOT right, or that someone else's perspective might be valid!

Today while reading Scripture, I read about how Jesus' parents brought him to the temple for the holy offering to God. A man named Simeon was there and he blessed Jesus. Then he went on to bless Mary and Joseph. In *Luke 2:33-35* Simeon said to Mary: "*This child marks both the failure and the recovery of many in Israel, a figure misunderstood and contradicted--the pain of a sword-thrust through you---*" (MSG).

This verse caused me to think about our current times. If Jesus was misunderstood and contradicted, what are the chances we will be too, especially if we are living lives to honor Him? Speaking from personal experience, the pain of betrayal and wrongful judgment can feel like a sword being thrust through our hearts, especially when it comes from those we love most dearly. The final line in this Scripture is what really hit me..."*But the rejection will force honesty, as God reveals who they really are."*

We are in a season when honesty seems like a thing of the past. When feelings and personal choice are more important than truth, and when standing for what is "right" is our right even if it's wrong.

So, that begs the question: Do we really want to live where truth no longer exists? Or do we want God to reveal who we are, what we are, and where we might have missed the mark? Don't we want honesty to be the one thing still treasured even if it means having to reject something or even be rejected? According to this Scripture, rejection forces honesty about the truth of who we are.

Therefore, I challenge us all: Reject lies that are told to discredit others. Reject that which injects strife and division. Reject anything that doesn't shout of God's glory because all these things are of Satan, the author of lies, division, and dishonesty.

In this journey called life, especially if we live for Jesus, we will most certainly be misunderstood and contradicted. We will feel the pain of a sword-thrust and we might even be rejected for telling the truth. There is a prize, for in the end, honesty will be revealed by God himself. He will bring about the big reveal and when he does, all truth will be clear and misunderstandings and contradictions will be laid to rest! When that happens, the pain of misunderstanding and rejection will have been worth it!

Motherhood

Watching her, I couldn't seem to blink back the tears welling in my eyes. My little girl was expecting a child of her own. Seeing her bulging stomach as her little boy grew inside, I wondered where the time had gone. How could she have grown into a woman so soon.

It seemed like only yesterday when I watched her adoringly follow her big brother Tucker around the house, mimicking his every move. I recall her feisty spirit as she rescued little brother Josh from the ball pit at Chuck E. Cheese when bigger boys had buried him. I remember her sailing down the irrigation ditch, floating on sleds with her best friend Megan; and her determination when she swam all one hundred laps during the swim-a-thon event.

Now we are waiting for her son to be born. I'll admit, I've chewed off my fingernails thinking about it. I'm so excited and yet, nervous. Soon she will be a mama and the little girl that has been my princess will transform. Gone are the bedtime stories, the back rubs, and quiet lullabies in the rocking chair. I can see her doing the same with her son. Again, those tears threaten to spill.

As the torch of motherhood moves to the next generation, I can't help but wonder: Did I do enough to prepare her? Will she mind if I still think of her as my baby? Will she have too many of those "I'll never do that like my mother" thoughts? Probably, but regardless, the sands of time have shifted. I dare not let my mind wander too far into the future. Even though we've had months to think and prepare, it's hard to imagine her with a child. Yet, it is going to happen, and soon.

Tonight, she's home relaxing as labor seems close. I'd love to give her one more back rub, to lay in the dark next to her and visit a bit. Tomorrow, it could all change. Tomorrow she could be holding her own son. She will know a joy that can only be known by a mother. She will understand how you would throw yourself in front of a car if it meant saving your child. She will realize the fear of a fever, the pain of an owwie, and the way your heart melts with a simple smile. She will feel the level of defense that will rise up inside if someone makes fun of or hurts her son's feelings. She will understand how deeply one can love another, simply because they are your child.

Tomorrow she could be starting the most exciting role of her life, with a new understanding of how deeply she's been loved all these years. She might be overwhelmed, realizing the weight of responsibility that comes with having a child.

A new chapter begins. As we turn the page, I thank God for my daughter, and for the joy of being part of her life as she moves into motherhood. I recognize that as much as I love her, God loves her even more, another lesson that motherhood teaches.

Before we say our goodnights, I will give her one more kiss as my baby, because tomorrow, she could be holding a baby of her own. What a joy to witness my own daughter become a mother, maybe even by tomorrow.

Psalm 127:3 "Behold, children are a heritage from the LORD, the fruit of the womb a reward." (ESV).

Sweet and Sour

It wasn't the first time in the past two months, and it certainly wouldn't be the last. Slipping into bed, a sour smell followed me, reminding me our grandson had upchucked his bottle on me twice. Then, when I failed to get the fresh diaper back on fast enough, I received a pee shower. The lingering fragrances of the day were sour, but sweet too.

With our children raised, it had been some time since we'd had a baby in our home. As a mother, I couldn't get my fill of babies. If it had been up to me, we'd have had a house full. After much struggle and loss, we were blessed with the privilege of raising three children. Now, by an amazing miracle, we were helping raise our grandson.

I loved the sweetness of this new baby. Sometimes in the early morning, his mama would lay him in bed between Ron and I as she got ready for work. I could watch him sleep for hours. When she looked at him, his eyes would soften as if adoring her face. What a special bond they had. She made me so proud, watching her as a mother to her son. Equally fun to watch was the growing relationship between him and his teenage uncle Josh, who begged to hold or feed him. Funny how Josh never wanted to help with the diaper change. What's with that?

The daily snuggles, smiles, and giggles gave us precious reminders of days long ago when we had babies of our own. I loved to watch the sweet smile creep across his face as he dozed off to sleep. When his mommy worked late, I loved being able to feed him the last bottle of the night. Putting him against my chest and patting his back for a burp, he'd fall fast asleep, leaving his soft rhythmic breath on my neck. It was impossible to put him down, so I'd often rock him long after he'd fallen asleep.

As I held this precious grandson, I realized something in my heart changed. When our own last two children were infants, they were our foster children. As much as we loved them, there lingered a dread that we might not get to keep them. It felt a bit like we were on a tightrope as we balanced our complete love with some sort of caution, just in case our hearts would be broken should these babies not remain with us.

Holding my grandson, it felt like something was breaking free. This baby, our first grandson, would forever be ours. We never had to consider he'd be anything but part of our family. We could anticipate days ahead, watching him grow up, even from these early stages of infancy. What a sweet and amazing thought!

The joy of his life in ours seemed to heal the fractures of uncertainty that were created so long ago, fractures I wasn't even aware were there. So, with the scent of sour milk on my skin, I closed my tired eyes, grateful for the sweetness of a new baby, which couldn't be more accurately described than in God's own Word: *"Grandchildren are the crown of the aged." Proverbs 17:6 (ESV).*

Falling Together

It promised to be a fun weekend, starting with a Christian concert followed by a trip to Helena. My dear friend Kelly had given me two tickets months ago for my birthday. In the busyness of life, I hadn't invited someone to use the second ticket, but at this final hour, time to make invites had passed. Rushing out the door, I joined Kelly and a few other friends for dinner.

After a fun dinner, we headed to the concert. Walking in the church door, I overheard a woman talking on the phone while a group of women waited around her. She said, "Well, we thought we had an extra ticket but..." I walked up to her and said, "Excuse me. Do you need another ticket?"

A startled expression accompanied her "Yes!".

"Well, here you go. God must have meant this for you." I handed her the ticket and rejoined my friends. It's not too often a group of women are speechless, but their stunned stares were a priceless reward for God allowing me to be part of His surprise.

After the concert, although I told myself I wouldn't buy any CD's, I found myself at the sales table where I bought three CD's. Talk about self-control! Back at home by 10:30 pm, I began planning out the next day's events which included a three-hour drive to Helena to attend my niece's bridal shower, followed by a dedication ceremony for my god-sister Heather. She had just purchased an assisted living facility, a fulfillment of her lifelong dream. She asked if I would help her dedicate it to the Lord. Before heading to bed, I found a couple appropriate verses.

An unexpected night shift for our daughter created a sleepover with our infant grandson, so I attended to bottle feedings at 1:30 and again at 5:30. After a quick shower and breakfast, I hit the road.

Enroute to Helena, I popped one of the new CDs from the previous night's concert into the player and let the music flow. As I listened, two songs seemed very appropriate for the dedication. My mind began thinking about how to play the songs without a CD player. I remembered throwing my iPad in the car at the last minute. Perhaps I could find the songs on the internet and play them off that.

Still pondering the details, I arrived at the bridal shower and enjoyed time with my nieces. Several hours later, I headed back down the road to the dedication, armed with my two scriptures and two songs. Arriving at Heather's, I discovered my iPad only had 20% battery left and no power cord to charge it. However, I happened to have my projector in the car along with the iPad adapter. I thought it out, hoping that if I plugged the iPad into the projector, maybe I could keep it going. Plus, we would have the benefit of speakers. So it went, as if planned to the absolute detail. Heather was pleased and God was honored as we gave glory to Him for Heather's residents and her fulfilled dream. Just as the last song ended, my iPad gave me the 5% power warning and shut down.

Who could imagine with so little preparation, it would turn out so perfect? The concert led to the beautiful music for the dedication. My drive to Helena gave me time to hear it and thus find it, and God provided the right equipment to be in place long enough to complete the dedication.

Sometimes God's plans are better achieved when we haven't made all the arrangements; when we wait with empty willing hearts seeking His direction. *Revelations 1*:8 describes Him as *"the Alpha and Omega, the beginning and the end." (KJV).* If we let Him fill in the middle, often it will fall together, bringing Him glory for the unexpected results.

Awe God

Time Well Spent

The day started out with plans to go to the pool; only to learn it closed for the summer. With only three days left of summer, it was disappointing. Trying to think of a way to salvage the last days of summer, I confirmed no one had any commitments until Friday, when school would begin and when I needed to fly to Seattle for a family reunion. My mind whirled trying to think of what we could do for the next three days. Awe, yes, Mount Rushmore, although five hours away, we could do that.

I had errands to run so on my way out the door, I announced to the family we were heading to Mount Rushmore and thus, they should be packed in two hours when I returned. My announcement brought stares and gaping jaws. Just in case they thought I was kidding, I added, "That's what I want for my birthday" just two days away. Several hours later, when I arrived home, much to my surprise, both Josh and Kassi were packed, ready to go with Finnigan. Even more surprising, my homebody husband said, "Well, if that's what you really want to do for your birthday, then I'm ready too." We loaded up and headed down the road.

The next three days were a blur of fun as we filled our time with new family memories. Ron teased me about driving so far for my birthday celebration and added how much he looked forward to payback time with his next birthday! We all had to admit, we enjoyed our perfect end to the summer.

Back home on Thursday evening, the kids readied themselves for school while I put my clothes through the laundry, plucked my brows, and packed for my morning flight to Seattle. As Ron dropped me at the airport the next morning, I'm pretty sure I heard the tires squeal as he drove off. Sometimes my spontaneity in this journey of life created a bit too much excitement for him.

Seattle meant another three days packed with activities as I enjoyed celebrating my aunt and uncle's 50th wedding anniversary. An extra bonus included treasured moments with my son Tucker and five-year-old granddaughter Leena. When it came time for our goodbyes, Leena relayed her feelings: "Can you stay forever Grandma?"

Trying to hide my own tears, I responded, "I'd love to, but I need to go home. We can always talk on the phone."

"It's not the same," Leena's face grew long as tears streamed down her cheeks. She was right, and I felt the pain in saying goodbye too.

As I boarded the plane, I thought of the past six crazy days, a road trip, sight-seeing, eating out, sleeping in a cramped hotel, flying to the west coast, enjoying time with our family, hellos, and goodbyes. We'd been doing life, even if it was a bit unplanned, unpredictable, and challenging.

Paul's perspective is relayed in *Philippians 1:22-26:* *"As long as I'm alive in this body, there is good work for me to do…So I plan to stay around awhile, companion to you as your growth and joy in this life of trusting God continues. You can start looking forward to a great reunion when I come visit you again." (MSG).*

His words remind me that in the limited time we have here on earth, there is good work to do. It's about taking in each moment and living life to its fullest, appreciating the things that make us laugh or cry, while doing whatever it takes to help each other grow in our relationship with one another and with God.

Someday there will come a final goodbye, an end to the time given in this life. For those we leave behind, in Leena's words, "it won't be the same". In the time left, we want our life to be full and our journey to point others toward the greatest reunion of all time, with our Lord Jesus Christ.

Behind the Scenes

The guest speaker at the family church camp worked with foster children. Since I was writing a book about the foster care crisis in our country, I wanted to hear his perspective. As is often the case, I left home later than intended. By the time I'd made the hour and a half drive to the camp and parked, church services had already started.

Making our way to the chapel, we could hear singing coming from inside. Finding a seat, I settled in as the speaker started. Whew! Just in time! Minutes into his presentation, he gave an assignment to pray silently over a verse for the next fifteen minutes. I'll admit, I felt disappointed, not that I'm opposed to prayer, but in my rush to leave, I didn't have my Bible with me, leaving me a bit ill-prepared. Besides, I came specifically to hear him speak!

Kassi and grandson Finnigan had traveled with me. They waited outside since Finn kept life busy. Gathering my purse, I exited and joined them. We decided to wander toward the children's area where all the children would be playing during the church service. We could surely find toys for Finnigan to entertain himself.

As we approached, we could hear a baby crying. Entering the cabin, we observed two young adults caring for five babies. Each held a baby which left two babies playing quietly and another who cried, expressing his unhappiness. As Finn found toys, I offered to be an extra set of arms to hold the crying baby.

The young lady looked at me with relief, "You don't mind?"

"Of course not, I'm happy to."

The little guy continued crying, even as I tried all the positions and tricks I knew. Finally, he called it quits and fell asleep, slung over my arm. For the duration of the service, I dared not move him from that position as he slept, even though my arm had become numb.

After the parents came to gather their children, I thought of how God often uses us behind the scenes. That baby's parents had no idea their infant was upset, but God knew and arranged for an extra set of hands to be in the nursery. It caused me to reflect on the many times the "behind the scenes" people are needed. The stage crew who puts all the details into a play that make it so successful, the waterboys who make sure athletes don't get dehydrated during the big game, the crew who arrives ahead of the band to set up the equipment for the concert. What about the great crowd of witnesses referred to in Hebrews 12:1. Talk about being behind the scenes!

Yes, we need the front-runners, the leaders, the stars, and the great speakers, but they couldn't do it without those who take care of the hundreds of details behind the scenes. At the end of the day, as we loaded into the car to drive home, I wasn't all that disappointed. I didn't get to hear the great speaker, but I did get the honor of working behind the scenes for the great Creator.

Hebrews 12:1 "Therefore, since we are surrounded by so great a cloud of witnesses, let us also lay aside every weight, and sin which clings so closely, and let us run with endurance the race that is set before us." (ESV).

The Labyrinth

It had been a fun weekend retreat with friends, a get away from life, and a time of reflection and inspiration. As we headed toward the final morning's wrap up "ceremony", I learned it would be held at a mountainside labyrinth. Approaching the area, I felt intrigued and yet, uneasy. When our host Sue asked us to step inside the circle of rocks, I complied. Immediately, my heart started pounding rapidly. As she began describing what we were going to do, including praying to seven different things, like the trees, the east, the west, etc., my uneasiness grew. Then as she described how we were going to make an offering, my heart began pounding so hard, I thought I might pass out. This conflicted with my Christian faith and I knew I could not participate. It would be an offense against God to pray or make an offering to anyone or anything but Him.

As Sue passed the offering around the group, she paused in front of me, inviting me to take the grain. "I'm sorry," I said, "but as a Christian, this is something I can't participate in." She moved on and began praying. Without any thought or plan, I began quietly praying aloud to God. I felt such a powerful need to pray for covering in what felt like a spiritual assault. Within seconds, Sue paused and turned her attention to me. "You are distracting me. Would you please move away?"

Stepping outside of the circle, my racing heart immediately quieted. With the dramatic physical change, I couldn't help but think of Jonah. When Jonah tried to run away from God, he boarded a ship only to have God create a terrible storm. Once the crew threw Jonah overboard, the storm immediately quieted (Jonah 1:15). I had just experienced my own storm. Outside of God's will, my heart pounded a warning. The moment I heeded the warning and stepped away from the occult, and back toward God, the storm in my heart calmed.

As I quietly prayed at a distance, I felt such sadness for those who remained. This labyrinth experience probably seemed harmless to them, but to me, it was like watching innocent lambs being led to slaughter, clearly unaware of their offense against God. It represented that tiny, one-degree step off the path to a destination that can slowly take us in the wrong direction, a direction away from the one true God.

As the "ceremony" concluded, I hurried to my car and headed home. In the quiet of the car, I began to cry, feeling such sadness over what I had just witnessed. Then God gave me an amazing reminder, Christ is the light of the world. When I began praying, bringing Christ into the setting, the enemy couldn't continue. Sue actually had to ask me to leave before she could proceed with her ceremony. Even with a tiny light of prayer, Christ was there and thus, the darkness couldn't remain, just like a lit candle being brought into a dark room, light overpowers and darkness dissipates.

Reflecting on the labyrinth experience was a bit unnerving, but I'm glad I witnessed it. It gave me an awareness of the subtle ways the enemy is at work in our world. It served as a warning to be alert. Perhaps, by taking a stand, the others will question why and seek answers. As we war for righteousness in a culture which seems to be turning away from God, we all need to be careful not to be led astray by what seems innocent. The true test is, if it doesn't honor God, then it is not of God, and we don't want anything to do with it.

"Be alert and of sober mind. Your enemy the devil prowls around like a roaring lion looking for someone to devour." 1 Peter 5:8. (NIV). The enemy's methods to devour might be very subtle, like a quiet mountainside labyrinth, so stay alert!

I Can Only Imagine

Barb had been in and out of our lives through the years as she moved around with her jobs. When she retired, she moved back to Helena to be close to the only people she considered family. My mom was one of them.

As Barb neared the end of her life, Mom became her caregiver. One day while visiting Mom, I had an opportunity to chat with Barb. She was resting on the couch, so I pulled up a chair to sit next to her. Barb didn't believe in God so I knew I needed to bring up the "God" subject. I hesitated though, because as Barb's pain had grown, she'd become short-tempered and conversations were a bit prickly.

I took a deep breath. "Barb, I don't want you to leave this world without knowing about God." Her response came out with a spat, "Well, if there's a God, where is He now? Why isn't He helping me now?"

Without thinking, I responded a bit more defensively than I intended, "Have you ever considered Mom is God's way of helping you?" Barb seemed at a loss for words and I knew the conversation had ended.

Soon after, Mom asked our pastor if he could visit with Barb to discuss final arrangements. He shared his faith and later relayed that Barb made a decision to ask Jesus into her life.

Barb died a few weeks later. I went back to Helena to help Mom with the funeral arrangements. We decided to include a relatively new song, "I Can Only Imagine" by MercyMe. My sister Colleen had a CD of it and would bring it with her when she came for the funeral (yes, there were days before modern day streaming and Pandora).

The day of the funeral, a horrific snowstorm moved in, creating white-out conditions. Mom's phone rang. When she answered, I quickly realized Colleen was on the other end. They made the wise decision that she shouldn't risk traveling on the roads.

As Mom continued her conversation with Colleen, I realized we'd need to find another copy of the song or decide on another song. Mom had a wonderful selection of older music from her era. Perhaps she had a good alternative.

I sat down in the old creaking rocking chair to look over her music. Picking up a CD, I realized it had "I Can Only Imagine" on it. Who would have guessed Mom was so hip? Such joy to once again recognize how God provided exactly what we needed.

So, just as planned, Barb's very intimate funeral included "I Can Only Imagine". It seemed so fitting, and I couldn't help but wonder what Barb experienced as a new believer, just meeting Jesus.

In the years since Barb's passing, I've thought of how close she came to not meeting Him and how timid I'd been about telling her, knowing I'd receive pushback. *Ezekiel 3:18-21* reminds us it is our responsibility to warn others that if they don't turn from their sins, they will die. If we don't warn them, when they die, then it's our fault, but if they listen, we'll have saved a life.

In a time when the world seems a bit chaotic, sharing the Message of Jesus is even more important. In fact, it might be the only "important" thing we do. Be bold. Have the conversation. Don't worry about how they will respond. Reactions and responses aren't up to us. The only thing that matters is that we are obedient to God Almighty in sharing His Good News.

Traditions

Holidays hold so many fond memories of times with my grandma. As an amazing cook and hostess, she created a wonderful and festive mood in her home. On one particular holiday, years after she passed, I wrote her this letter, so I'd never forget.

Dear Grandma:

    I often think of you. So many holidays around your table, heaped with a feast of ham, holiday potatoes, green bean casserole, multiple side dishes, dinner rolls with jelly, and all the pickles, olives, and trimmings one could fathom. They were all canned from the garden or freshly baked in your kitchen. Okay, so maybe the olives weren't made by you, but that was the exception. We were all there, one big, happy family. We grew larger with marriage and children through the years and with each addition, you made each feel as if they always belonged with us.

    At your very table, on Mother's Day, we announced we were expecting a baby. We had just wrapped up a baby shower for Michael which you helped host. How you loved him, as well as the rest of our family. As was often the case when we sat for our meal, you asked me to say grace. I have no idea why, because when I prayed, I always cried. I guess we were all a bunch of saps who loved the emotion we felt and the joy of being together around your table. During that particular prayer, I added an extra thank you for the next baby due in November. Grandad broke down into tears first, and when everyone else realized what I just said, all followed suit. Two babies in seven months, after years of waiting. How we loved sharing our joys with you.

You created a safe warmth around your kitchen table where we shared big announcements and discussed matters of the heart, as you served homemade cookies and a can of Coke.

It's been decades since you went to be with the Lord and in the years that followed, the most remarkable thing happened. I became a grandma too. When I tell my little ones "I love you," I hear your tender voice in my mind. When my heart softens at the sight of them, I think of how evident it was that yours did too, whenever you saw us. As I snuggle and rock my grandbabies, I remember watching you do the same with my children.

I remember the Easter Egg hunts in your big yard, and how your face lit up with a wide smile when we brought our eggs to show you. We won't be having an Easter egg hunt this year. Leena isn't in Montana and Finnigan is too little, but it won't be long. When they show me their finds, I will remember you again and how wonderful you made me feel as your granddaughter.

You would have been a great-great grandma by now. Of all the titles you had in your life, this one seems most fitting, for you were indeed a great, great, wonderful grandma. I only hope I will have as lasting an impression on my grandchildren as you had on me.   Love, Denise

Esther 9:27-28 speaks of Jewish traditions and the importance of remembering. *"It became a tradition for them, their children, and all future converts to remember these two days every year on the specified dates set down in the letter. These days are to be remembered and kept by every single generation, every last family, every province and city. These days of Purim must never be neglected among the Jews; the memory of them must never die out among their descendants."* (MSG)

Grandma made traditions memorable. It's hard work to keep them going, but they create a thread through generations, tying values and beliefs back to God and family. Much like a tree root, traditions can give families a sense of stability, allowing for treasured occasions that are predictable and expected. I am so grateful to my Grandma for passing along wonderful traditions.

The Connection

Standing in the check-out line at Walmart, our two-year-old grandson Finnigan had me on my toes. Keeping what we'd selected in the cart proved to be challenging as our little man kept shuffling things from the shelf in and out of the cart. I glanced at the cashier as I instructed Finn to give the lady the toy, so she could ring it up. Almost immediately, I realized a man, not a lady, stood at the cash register. Embarrassed, I apologized.

He responded, "No problem. At least you acknowledged me."

His comment caught me by surprise, so I asked, "Doesn't that usually happen?"

"No, most people don't even look me in the eye."

In an attempt to make up for my bad behavior, I was determined to have a short conversation as he finished ringing up our groceries. When I left, I wished him a Merry Christmas and thanked him for his help.

In the weeks since that conversation, it hasn't left my mind. It's made me ponder: How often have I gone about life without making connections with others? Like at the gym while trying not to die on the treadmill? (Okay, so maybe that's understandable). Or when my children are talking, but my mind is miles away? Let's be honest, how many times have I been in a checkout line, absent-minded and distracted, not making eye contact with the cashier?

In this busy world, perhaps we all need a reminder to take time to connect. After all, Christ's journey to earth was all about connecting. He came to earth so we could know our Heavenly Father. He could have just given us a book to read (which we have in the Bible) or a movie to watch (there are plenty of those), but that wasn't enough. He wanted us to have a personal connection with God the Father.

"If you have known me, you would have known my Father also. From now on you do know him and have seen him. John 14:7 (ESV).

Connections matter. Without them, we can't impact others. We miss out on what God might be doing in us and for us. We squander opportunities to change and grow as others contribute to our lives. For all we know, the few moments we invest in connecting with others could be the slivers of time God will use to bring awareness to His greatness. Let's not miss that connection.

Be Still

Finding quiet time is something I've always struggled with, but I had a new experience that left me wondering.

My friend Sheri called, asking for a favor. Her sister Debi had suffered a horrific accident, leaving her in a light coma. It had been months since her accident and although hospitalized in Billings, I hesitated to go see her. I knew she only had brief moments of being "awake", so I didn't want to take time away from her family, but since Sheri lived in Washington, she asked if I could help. "Please go and pray over her. And would you read Scripture to her?" Of course I would. I had met Debi, but it had been a while since I last saw her. I wondered if she'd recognize me.

Sheri warned me, "It's hard to talk to someone who can't respond." With her words, I almost laughed. Years of being married to my sweet husband, who was much better at listening than talking, had given me much practice in talking to unresponsive people. Just kidding Ron, but seriously, one must admit, when it came to gifts and talents, I had been blessed exceedingly with the gift of gab. Part of that blessing included a man of few words who was a great listener!

On a more serious note, I had some experience being with unresponsive people. In my dad's final days of life, he slipped into a coma, so talking and reading the paper to him had been the last shred of communication with him. It brought comfort, so I knew there could be some comfort for Debi too.

Arriving at the hospital, I located Debi's room and entered. When I spoke, Debi opened her eyes. For the next forty-five minutes., I talked, prayed, and read Scripture. Most of the time,

Debi's eyes remained open as she watched me, and although she didn't respond, I thought of *Matthew 18:20: "For where two or more are gathered in my name, there am I among them." (ESV)*. I felt His Holy Spirit and I reminded her, "He is here with us Debi."

As our time passed, I began to feel a sense of wonder for what Debi might be experiencing in the quiet weeks, and now months that were passing. I wondered what God might be communicating to her in this season of silence. Could He have revealed the sound of the angelic choirs or the heavenly orchestra that might accompany them? Or perhaps He shared the joy of children's laughter as it reflected off the clouds? Or could the thunderous clap of a lightning storm sound completely different when filtered through the ears of God? Perhaps He even shared mysteries that are yet unknown to those of us who allow our heads to be cluttered with thoughts, demands, and schedules.

As I leaned to say goodbye, giving Debi a kiss on each cheek, one from me and one from Sheri, I reminded her of *Deuteronomy 31:8, "It is the Lord who goes before you. He will be with you; he will not leave you or forsake you. Do not fear or be dismayed." (ESV)*.

I can hardly wait until Debi can tell us what God revealed to her in her long season of quiet. When she is finally able to speak, she will have an amazing testimony. In the meantime, her silence blessed me because I can't help but wonder; what would God share with me if I would allow for quieter moments of stillness and silence in my life?

Downsizing

I'd been trying to convince my better half for several years that we needed to downsize. With the kids pretty much out of the house, the big house and half-acre yard demanded more work than we wanted, but the thought of moving was daunting in itself. Then our daughter Kassi called, asking if we'd be interested in selling the family home to her and her growing family. How could one say anything but YES? The idea of my grandchildren being raised in the home their mama had grown up in had sweet appeal.

  We quickly went to work looking for a smaller home with the goal of making the transaction before school started in mid-August. The housing market was tight, but we worked tirelessly with our realtor. As the weeks passed, I began to feel a bit anxious. Although I love my daughter and her family dearly, the idea of us all living together even for a short time would be challenging. They came with three dogs, six cats, three children, a very pregnant daughter, and her husband. It would be a bit tight if we had to share a roof.

  Moving needed to happen, but we also wanted to take a trip to Seattle to meet our newest granddaughter, Leila. So, over the Fourth of July weekend, we made the twelve-hour trip west. As we traveled, I mentioned to Ron we needed to make an offer on a house by July 15th if we were going to be able to make the move on time. We prayed about our need and asked God to provide it in the limited time we had.

  The joy of welcoming our newest granddaughter filled the next few days. Upon returning home from Seattle, we hit the house hunting process hard. Another discouraging day left us driving around, looking at neighborhoods without our realtor. Then we saw a "For Sale by Owner" sign in a yard of a newer subdivision with townhouses. We pulled over to the side of the road and placed the call. The owner could be there in fifteen minutes to show us the house.

It turned out to be perfect. The right size for our downsize, the right colors for our existing furniture, and best yet, fit in our price range. The next morning, we called the owner and made an offer. Although we tried to do a little negotiating, she told us two more people were coming to look that afternoon. In fact, she had just put the "For Sale" sign up hours before we called, so we were the first to see it. With that, we agreed to her price. She offered a handshake to seal the deal, but we insisted on giving her earnest money. Just as we had prayed, on July 15th, we negotiated a deal to buy our next home.

Mid-August arrived and the paperwork hadn't been finalized on Kassi's side, so we couldn't close on the new home. We called the owner and since she had already moved out, she allowed us to move in and simply asked we put the utilities in our name. When we finally signed the closing documents at the end of August, the owner told us she had prayed through our home with blessings for us. What a lovely gift to leave! Since Kassi's family had purchased our home, and our new home was significantly smaller, we left the excess furniture and belongings she could use, making downsizing and discarding much simpler.

God's providence was evident: from finding our house within hours of the sign being put up, making an offer before anyone else had looked at it, on the exact date needed to make the move happen, the owner's willingness to let us move in ahead of signing the papers, and her prayer for our family as she passed her home onto us with God's blessing.

Jeremiah 33:3 reminds us: *"Call to me and I will answer you; and will tell you great and hidden things that you have not known." (ESV)* Quite literally, God had hidden the perfect home so it would be ready to answer our specific need and time. He is such an amazing God.

The Gift of Time

Talk about chaotic. The year started out with being asked to run for the legislature, something I NEVER intended to do. My dad had served as a State Representative for eight years just prior to his death. That was plenty of politics for me, but I promised I'd pray about it. God led me to Isaiah and verse after verse seemed to encourage me to use the opportunity to elevate the foster care crisis in Montana. So, I agreed, but only after asking my family, especially daughter Kassi. She had gotten engaged on New Year's Eve, so we were planning a fall wedding. This was my priority. Kassi, along with the rest of my crazy family encouraged me.

We were off, trying to run a campaign while planning a wedding. In October, Kassi had a picture-perfect wedding and two weeks later, I lost the election. Thank you, Jesus! During the journey, I made some wonderful connections and friends, but God knew I didn't have time for it, especially with the news that followed a month later. Mom called to tell us the doctors diagnosed her with lung cancer. Mom, who never lost her fast pace as she kept up with all of us and our activities. Truth be known, with her energy, I figured she'd outlive me, but cancer, really? Dad died of lung cancer as it metastasized nearly five years after his colon cancer diagnosis, so we'd been here before.

Several weeks later, brother Dave and I were with Mom when the doctor confirmed she not only had cancer, but aggressive Mesothelioma. No long-term treatment and a prognosis of less than a year left us shocked.

Yet, we'd been given a gift of time. From then on, all of us planned special time with Mom. Dave organized a snowcat trip through Yellowstone Park with her long-time friend Carole and took oodles of road trips to fulfill her requests to see friends and attend to final details. Colleen organized a spa weekend for Mom, Colleen and me and we got to spoil her. Ron, Josh, and I took her to Cooke City to spend Christmas with Kassi's family and to Seattle for Easter to be with Tucker's family.

The grandkids organized a surprise birthday party, arriving in a limousine to pick her up with all nine adult grandchildren crammed in, and Mom was thrilled! Additionally, six family members moved, including us, so Colleen took Mom on road trips so she could see everyone's new digs. In between it all, Colleen's youngest son got married and three more great-grandchildren were born, filling Mom's quiver with nine grandchildren and twelve great-grands. What an amazing legacy!

As fall arrived, it was evident Mom could no longer live alone, so Colleen and Dave moved her to an assisted living facility in Bozeman where they both lived. Then we took shifts attending to her needs. What a gift to be able to care for Mom in her final season.

It was a crazy chaotic season of time, but by focusing on ways to create joy, there were so many happy days instead of dreading the loss ahead.

Psalm 90:12: "Teach us to number our days, that we may gain a heart of wisdom. & 14: Satisfy us in the morning with your unfailing love, that we may sing for joy and be glad all our days. & 16: Make us glad for as many days as you have afflicted us, for as many years as we have seen trouble. May your deeds be shown to your servants, your splendor to their children. May the favor of the Lord our God rest on us; establish the work of our hands for us— yes, establish the work of our hands." (NIV).

Yes, we'd been given the gift of time. Through the example of both our parents, we learned that although we must live with the cards we've been dealt, we can have joy in the journey. In their living and their dying, we gained hearts of wisdom as God's splendor was lived out through them.

Laboring

It was December 3rd, and my daughter Kassi was in labor. She had chosen to do an in-home delivery. Watching my daughter struggle to bring her daughter into the world created a personal pain I'd never experienced. I held her hand in a death grip as if to pass my own strength onto her. She was getting tired. Her eyes searched my face as a desperate cry escaped her lips. "Mom, I can't do this."

"Yes you can, honey. You're strong. You're almost there. You've got this. Your baby is almost here." Inside though, I wasn't as confident. "What if something was wrong? What if she truly couldn't do it?" I glanced toward the midwife, looking for assurance. She nodded without saying a word. I had no choice but to trust. We were too far into labor to get to a hospital now.

I started praying silently, but then paused when my daughter experienced another contraction. When she caught her breath, she whispered, "Keep praying Mom." Chills ran down my spine. I'd been praying silently. How could she have heard me? I began praying aloud. Then the most amazing thing happened. I had the privilege of praying our beautiful granddaughter Tilly into the world and praising God when she took her first breath.

Three weeks later, I found myself once again coaching through labor. This time though, I was trying to help my mother as she attempted to cross over into heaven. Mom's eyes were glued to mine. She could no longer speak, so I was doing my best to anticipate her needs. I held her hand, just like I had my daughter's weeks ago. "You've got this Mom; you can do this. You're almost there, go give Jesus a big hug." Inside though, everything in me wanted to crumble. Saying goodbye was going to be very hard. As the hours passed, Mom labored to free her spirit from her body. Then the most amazing thing happened. My siblings and I had the privilege of praying over her as she took her last breath and went to her heavenly home.

Laboring is a part of being born as well as a part of dying. It's also part of the season we call life. As a result of the original sin, in Genesis 3, God determined that man, by the sweat of his brow, would labor to work the ground to survive. For women, there would be painful labor in having children.

Labor is in day-to-day living. When the enemy tries to tell us we're not worthy, we must work to remind ourselves we belong to the King of Kings. When a loved one chooses hate and strife, we must labor to return love and turn the other cheek. It takes hard work to ward off the enemy's attacks. Equally difficult is doing the work of the Lord. Being a foster parent knowing there will be a painful goodbye. Venturing to a foreign country to serve orphans while abandoning the comforts of home. Serving food to the poor while recognizing food won't begin to satisfy their needs. Holding the hand of a parent who has buried their child, or praying over a sick friend who needs fresh hope.

In between the first breath and the last, we labor. It is in the labor where we leave a legacy for Christ, create joy and meaning, instilling values for the next generation. No matter how difficult it is, as long as we are laboring for the Lord, it will be worth it.

"Therefore, my dear brothers and sisters, stand firm. Let nothing move you. Always give yourselves fully to the work of the Lord, because you know that your labor in the Lord is not in vain." 1 Corinthians 15:58 (NIV).

"I press on toward the goal for the prize of the upward call of God in Christ Jesus." Philippians 3:14 (ESV).

Leave the Door Open

In the final week of Mom's life, even though her words were few and labored, regularly she would state, "Leave the door open." Funny thing is, her bedroom door remained open. Furthermore, she was seldom alone in her room, thus no reason to feel isolated. Yet, she would insist. We began to realize the door she intently watched wasn't the door to her room. Instead, her eyes focused on a corner in the room. Evidently, the door she observed was only visible from a spiritual perspective, as the curtain between life and death became more transparent. Perhaps this was her doorway to heaven.

    I couldn't help but stare whenever she mentioned the door. What did she see? Was light streaming through, or music and laughter floating in the air? Could she see the banquet table overflowing for the great feast? How I wanted to tiptoe to the doorway and peek through, perhaps even help Mom take her final step to the other side.

    Mom remained, unable to abandon her will to live. Sister Colleen reminded me, Mom never wanted to miss out. Three new great-grandchildren had arrived, and she hoped to meet them. Marriage proposals were anticipated as Mom wondered if her oldest granddaughter might receive a ring for Christmas. Grandson Sam's wedding was coming up in six months and Mom intended to dance at it. She didn't want to miss out on anything in this life, even while knowing the best was yet to come.

    Days passed as Dave, Colleen, and I assured her we would be okay, her work on earth was done, and thus, time for her reward. One evening heavenly visitors came through the door and Mom told me she needed to get packed, so she could get going. I encouraged her, suggesting they were here to help her move but still, she tarried. Then around noon one day, she went through the door, leaving behind her earthly body.

In the days since, I have often thought of her door. Doors are such practical and ordinary things meant to keep things in or out. We think of doors to enter everything from our homes, buildings, and cars, as well as entries into our eyes, minds, and hearts.

Yet, God uses doors to represent the extraordinary. Doorways were covered with lamb's blood thousands of years ago to keep death from entering, thus the celebration of Passover. There was the open door of the tomb and the stone rolled away. The missing body and the assumption that Jesus' body had been taken. Who could fathom or understand that He opened the door to leave and thus overcome death itself. Jesus described himself as a door: *"I am the door. If anyone enters in by me, he shall be saved." John 10:9 (ESV).*

Perhaps there are doors you've hidden behind, maybe for too long. Maybe your heart or mind has been closed to truths you can't or aren't willing to fathom. There might be things your eyes need to see if only you'd open them, or a door standing so blatantly open, yet, you just can't will yourself through it. Now might be a good time to make your move, open your mind, your heart, or your eyes, because there is one door you don't want to miss. The door to our Savior. He's standing there, waiting for you, and all you have to do is open it!

"Here I am! I stand at the door and knock. If anyone hears my voice and opens the door, I will come in and eat with him, and he with me." Revelations 3:20 (NIV).

The Loan

As I stood surveying Mom's belongings, I felt a bit overwhelmed with the many treasures of my sweet mama. She had recently passed away and now remained the tremendous task of determining what we kept. Brother Dave had already done a lot of leg work, but as we sorted through a pile of papers, I noticed an unmarked envelope. I took a moment to open it and look inside. When I saw the contents, my heart quickened and tears rushed my eyes.

My mind snapped back to nearly thirty years ago. After our daughter Amy's stillbirth, while at work, a co-worker asked me to come to her office. When I got there, she directed me to the closet where a tattered slick piece of yellowed paper hung. "I think this was meant for you to have," she said as she removed it from the wall and handed it to me. On it was printed a poem called "The Loan". In the months of grief that followed, the poem gave me great comfort as I read and reread it and then tucked it into Amy's treasure box along with her hospital blanket and bracelet. Several months after Amy's stillbirth, our son Michael died of SIDS. We intended to adopt him, but when he was a month old, his birth mother changed her mind and reclaimed him. Five months later, we received word that he too had died. We were devastated. A friend sent me a copy of his funeral notice. On the inside cover was printed "The Loan", the same poem my friend had given me from the office closet.

Several decades after our children's passing, my dear friend Susan called. Her grandson had just passed away. She wondered if I still had the poem and asked if I would send it to her. I offered her a copy, but she requested the original. I wrestled with giving it away. It felt like it belonged to my children, but that was selfish. Susan had been part of our journey back then, even hosting a baby shower for Michael. She had been a source of comfort in our days of grief that followed. The fact Susan still remembered the yellowed poem meant it was time to pass it along. So, I took a copy and relinquished the original, hoping it would help her in her season of grief, just like it had for me in mine.

    Now, sorting through Mom's treasures, inside this envelope was another original of "The Loan", printed on the same slick paper, only this one wasn't tattered nor yellowed. Had my brother opened that envelope, he'd have had no idea the value. For me, it would become one of my greatest treasures from my mother's belongings. It was a reminder to be grateful for the gift of the loan of another of God's children, my mother.

The Loan

"I'll lend you for a little time a child of mine," God said;
"For you to love while he lives
and mourn for when he's dead.
It may be six or seven years, or twenty-two or three.
But will you, 'till I call him back, take care of him for me?
He'll bring his charms to gladden you,
and shall his stay be brief.
You'll have his lovely memories as solace for your grief.
I cannot promise he will stay, since all from earth return.
But there are lessons taught down there
I want this child to learn.
I've looked the wide world over in search of teachers true.
And from the throngs that crowd life's lanes,
I have selected you.
How will you give him all your love,
not think the labor vain?
Nor hate me when I come to take him back again?
I fancied that I heard them say: "Dear Lord, Thy will be done!" For all the joy Thy child shall bring,
the risk of grief we'll run.
We'll shelter him with tenderness.

*We'll love him while we may.
And for all the happiness we've known,
forever grateful stay.
But shall the angels call him much sooner than we've planned.
We'll brave the bitter grief that comes,
and surely understand."
Author Unknown.*

Denise E. Johnson

Ripping Away

A week after my husband Ron's heart catheter procedure, the sticky bandage still clung tightly to his thigh. We needed to check the wound, so the sticky bandage needed to come off. Although he'd been tremendously shaved prior to the procedure, men simply have too much hair and their bodies weren't meant for being taped, waxed, or otherwise made bare. Leaving that sticky bandage on much longer was only going to compound the problem.

As we discussed how to remove the sticky bandage, great resistance came from Ron. It's not like I enjoy seeing him in pain, but sometimes we simply must do what needs to be done. Motherhood prepares one for moments like this. So, in one quick movement, I ripped it off, just as he cried out, begging me, "Don't rip it! Don't rip it!"

Moments later, there was a knock on our bedroom door. College age son Josh reminded us "we have neighbors"! Evidently, the whole fiasco had caused our son great embarrassment, especially when we realized, yes indeed, the window was open for all to hear! Gee, without even trying, we had once again embarrassed one of our children! Isn't parenting fun?

As Josh closed the door, Ron assured me he'd never forgive me, but as soon as he caught his breath, we found ourselves laughing hysterically. Yes indeed, what had the neighbors thought in hearing Ron's desperate and loud pleas to, "not rip it"?

As God often does, he uses these moments to teach. Ron's bandage had served its purpose, but with that accomplished, it being stuck to his skin wasn't going to improve the situation. I couldn't help but ponder other things that can get us stuck: Bad circumstances, jobs, or relationships.

God doesn't want us stuck; He wants us growing, healing, and moving toward Him. If people, positions, habits, or circumstances are creating stumbling blocks in our growth toward God and what He has created us to do, no matter how painful it might be, we might have to rip some things out of our lives. *2 Timothy 3:1-5* is a good reminder: *"But understand this, that in the last days there will come times of difficulty. For people will be lovers of self, lovers of money, proud, arrogant, abusive, disobedient to their parents, ungrateful, unholy, heartless, unappeasable, slanderous, without self-control, brutal, not loving good, treacherous, reckless, swollen with conceit, lovers of pleasure rather than lovers of God, having the appearance of godliness, but denying its power. Avoid such people."* (ESV). In *John 15*, Jesus gives the analogy of a gardener pruning away dead or unfruitful branches.

We often call this "setting boundaries". Like most people, I've had to make the hard choice to separate myself from toxic people and circumstances. Even when people are abusive or circumstances are not beneficial, creating boundaries can be very painful. They are important though because as *Proverbs 22:24-25* states, *"Make no friendship with man given to anger, nor go with a wrathful man, lest you learn his ways and entangle yourself in a snare."* (ESV). Equally important is the reminder in *Matthew 5:44: "But I tell you, love your enemies and pray for those who persecute you."* (NIV).

There is comfort in praying. We can't hate someone when we are praying for them. We can't grow bitter about a circumstance if we're praying over it. And so I pray, because God can repair and restore anything or anyone that has had to be ripped away, making it something that is better than before.

Denise E. Johnson

Day at the Beach

Such a beautiful day to head to the beach. Gathering the beach toys, towels, sunscreen, and suits, the family headed out. They couldn't wait to get their feet in the sand. As their mom unloaded the car, the kids ran with great enthusiasm toward the water. Mom followed. She stretched out the blankets and stuck the umbrella in the sand. Glancing up she saw her darlings splashing and laughing. They all needed this break. After positioning all the beach gear, she plopped onto a beach towel. Again, she looked out at her children. The littlest had floated too far out. She stood, shielded her eyes, raised her hand to wave the children back and shouted, "Come back!" Big brother heard her and pulled his little brother closer to shore. Playful laughter filled the air.

    Mom paused to rub sunscreen on her arms. Glancing toward the water she once again called out to her darlings. "Come closer to the shore. Don't get too far out." Again, they responded by moving closer to the shore. She began to relax as she watched the children play. She opened the book she'd brought to read. Soon, enjoying the warmth of the sun, she became engrossed in the book. A shriek caused her to jump to her feet. Her children had strayed too far out. They were in over their heads. She stood and without moving a muscle, watched as they drifted out to the ocean.

    What? Are you kidding? That isn't what a mother would do! Any mother would get up and race out into the water to carry her children back to safety as would any good father. None of us can fathom a parent who would stand at the shores and watch their children succumb to the ocean without making any effort to save them.

Many feel a bit like those children, struggling to keep our noses above water. Somehow in the process of filling our bank accounts, working our important jobs, and enjoying leisure time with our hobbies, we lost sight of the shore. It didn't happen because we lacked a good parent who warned us, but rather because we didn't listen and come back when we still could. Instead, we bobbed along, drifting away while building our own small empires without thought of the warning to stay close to our protector. In our arrogant pride, we didn't heed the warning.

Like a good mother at the shore, God has been standing calling out, "Come back. It is safer next to me where I will love and protect you." It is His desire for us to be close to Him. You might ask: If that's His desire, why doesn't he protect us? Why would He allow bad things to happen? Well, because he loves us enough to allow us to make our own choices; choices that often affect others, some for good, others for harm.

If you find yourself like the child beyond the reach of his mother's hands, just remember, God has a lifeboat. He sent His own Son to give his life in exchange for yours. As a result, you can come under the shelter and safety of God for all eternity. It's your choice. Will you reach out to the hand extending from the boat? Will you set aside your own agenda long enough to consider it might not be God's? In reality, we can't survive the challenges of life without God any more than children can survive at the ocean without their mother. Choose well, because the freedom to choose is a gift in itself. Life without choices would be like the world without oceans. God is a good Father who is ready to pull you back to Him.

Isaiah 44:22: "Return to Me, for I have redeemed you." (NIV).

Denise E. Johnson

And That's the Truth

Is there any greater joy than being a parent? The sweet smile of recognition that comes across their face when you pick them up from their crib. The reflection of yourself or your spouse when their expressions remind you of one another. The joy you feel over their achievements whether it is watching them take their first steps or graduate from high school. We feel ownership of our children. The fact they are our children is irrefutable, a truth that cannot be disputed. Even if the smartest, most respected person you know told you otherwise, they would be wrong. Your children are completely your children.

I've had the joy of being a parent and knowing the lengths I'd go to defend my children. I've also had the privilege of watching my children, nieces, and nephews experience the joy of raising their own children. Such an amazing time when children are young and can be naive to the snags of life that could distract or harm them, especially in today's culture where truth seems to be a moving target.

Today, truths are often diluted to opinion, feelings, perspectives, and twisted confusion. We hear phrases like: "That's your truth" or, "You can believe that if you want." If we need confirmation for "our truth", all we need to do is go to social media or a news channel. We can believe something that is complete nonsense while not believing something that is right in front of our face. In both cases, belief has nothing to do with the truth. However, if we listen to the false narratives long enough, we can lose sight of what is truly true.

Truth can be complicated. Sometimes the truth hurts or we simply don't want to accept it. To top it off, as humans we tend to be a bit arrogant. We think if we say or think something, it IS, even when it isn't. Truth is the greatest gift we can give someone, because the truth withheld is more painful. Deception is, in fact, cruel. Yet, we sometimes are willing to be deceived because we simply can't or don't want to accept the truth. Regardless of our reaction to the truth, the truth remains TRUTH.

In this time in our nation, many are trying to find their voice, their purpose, their cause. They stand with a microphone in their hand or act in ways to draw attention, seemingly unaware they've missed the point; the truth that would bring them joy, peace, a fresh perspective, and freedom. Far beyond the riots, the politics, the racial rhetoric, passions or causes, is a truth far greater.

What is that truth? Well, it's simple. God sent His only Son to die for YOU. God loved YOU so much He didn't think the world would be complete without YOU. YOU are His child, so loved by Him that He made a way for you to spend eternity in heaven. Whether you believe it or not, that's the truth. Don't miss out on the most important truth you could ever experience.

John 8:32: "And you will know the truth; and the truth will set you free." (ESV).

Denise E. Johnson

Genealogy – YAWN!

Many people love to study and track genealogy, but to be completely honest, I find it to be a bit of a bore. I do enjoy the unique stories like the one from my husband's side, where his grandmother's family missed their ship coming to America, the Titanic. The scandalous or mysterious stories which give personality and understanding to our ancestors are interesting, but the long list of names and dates are a yawner for me.

Even when I read the Bible, I skip through the long genealogical lists. However, the one for Jesus in Matthew 1 has always intrigued me. Why didn't God include Jesus, who became the Highest Priest, in the genealogical Levite line of priests? Furthermore, why was Joseph's lineage listed when he wasn't even Jesus' biological father. Scripture says, *"Jacob the father of Joseph, the husband of Mary, was the mother of Jesus who is called the Messiah." Matthew 1:16 (NIV)*.

Today, I had a light bulb moment while reading the Message translation of *Hebrews 7:14, "there is nothing in Jesus' family tree connecting him with that priestly line."* To sum it up, God was intentional in leaving Jesus out of the genetic line of priests. The old priesthood had failed and through Jesus, *"a new way that does work brought us right into the presence of God"*. Jesus was left out so there would be no connection to the old priesthood. None, a fresh start, a new beginning.

On the other hand, Joseph was intentionally included. As the mother of adopted children, that makes sense to me because Joseph was, in every sense, Jesus' father without prejudice of genealogical lineage or blood lines, just as our adopted children are ours.

This caused me to think of the idea of God's intention, and I realized that just as God intentionally created situations for Jesus, He has intentionally done the same for us. It is no accident we are alive today, in this season of time, with the family we are in, with the past history, and future promise ahead. Our physical appearance, personality, and purpose have all been intentionally designed by God.

God has also intentionally left things out of our lives because it's not His will. If I try to pursue them, I will waste my time and energy on things that don't honor God. Yet even when I go after the wrong things, He is faithful to give me the resources, tools, knowledge, and support to realign my life with Him. First, I need to recognize I've strayed so I can repent and humble myself enough to learn the lesson.

Just as God is intentional in what He chooses to include or exclude from our lives, we need to be intentional in what we do and don't do. For me that has meant spending more time in God's Word while putting healthy boundaries around divisive, toxic agendas and people. It's meant praying and seeking counsel so the emotional side of me doesn't lose sight of God's purpose and plan.

In this journey of life, I want to be intentional about being aware of God's purposes so that I'm not distracted and drawn away. We can't afford to be sucked into sin, divisions, and conflict. There is too much kingdom work that needs to be done. With Jesus' death, God overhauled the old covenant and replaced it with a new one. There is no greater message or cause to share than the Good News of Jesus Christ. Be intentional about telling others about Him.

"Christ was sacrificed once to take away the sins of many; and he will appear a second time, not to bear sin, but to bring salvation to those who are waiting for him." Hebrews 9:28 (NIV)

Denise E. Johnson

Suddenly Moments

I love it when I stumble upon a word or series of words in Scripture that causes me to pause and reflect. Recently, I noticed the word "Suddenly". Of course, I had to look it up. Defined as "quickly, swiftly, without warning". Not surprisingly, it's a word used frequently in Scripture.

When the angel appeared to the Shepherds, he was there suddenly. Suddenly a fierce storm struck the lake when the disciples were in a boat with Jesus. Thinking of these times, I pondered the times in my life when "suddenly" changed everything. Like when we wanted to have a baby. Four years passed then suddenly I was pregnant. Another time, exhausted from running a restaurant for years, suddenly we received a call from someone who wanted to buy it. When we learned Mom had terminal cancer, suddenly we knew our time with her was short. In each circumstance, life had quickly changed.

It seems like there is always a season of waiting. We wait for test results, election results, a promotion, the holidays, a big sale, a proposal, a vacation, and on and on. Waiting is hard, right? We want to know what's next. We want to move on. Better yet, we want our wait to end with our desired outcome. At some point, quite suddenly, it will be over. Suddenly we'll know and we will move forward based on what we learn.

Many seasons in our life are redefined by "suddenly" moments. That's what happened for Mary when she learned she would carry the Christ child. Her suddenly moment didn't mean things would become easier. In fact, just the opposite. With the knowledge, things were clearer. Mary knew without a doubt God was with her, literally, carrying Him inside her.

God is with us too if only we seek Him. Our suddenly moments are of no surprise to Him. He's known about them from the beginning of time. They can be good news or bad news, but they often come after a season of waiting. Most of us aren't good at waiting, but waiting can be a time to rest, reprioritize, and refresh. A time to allow God to help us work through solutions and reactions His way.

No wait lasts forever. Suddenly our answer will come. When it does, we can find comfort in knowing He's had a plan laid out all along. Let's use our seasons of waiting to lean into God so when our suddenly moment happens, even if it isn't the result we want, our responses will bring Him honor and glory.

Psalm 27:14 "Wait for the LORD, be strong, and let your heart take courage; wait for the LORD!" (ESV).

Denise E. Johnson

Did You Get the Message?

As I pulled into the driveway of my daughter's home, our granddaughter Irene saw me first. Her face lit up and she turned and ran toward me as fast as her little two-year-old legs would carry her. As soon as she reached me, I scooped her up and we exchanged BIG BEAR hugs. Right on her heels, big brother Finn embraced my legs with his four-year-old arms. "Nanny," they cried out together. A sweet swoon accompanied their voices which made my heart melt. Irene's face beamed as her deep dimple enunciated her smile. She pulled my hair away from my ears to look at my earrings. She loved to look at them. Big brother quickly lined out the expectations of the visit as he urged me along. "Can you push me on the swing?"

Carrying Irene, we mounted the steps to the house, crossed the kitchen and were soon in the backyard. Finn pointed out the pumpkin plants growing in the garden while Irene leaned toward the swing with her own agenda, "My turn." Soon both children were settled in their swings. Irene's golden blonde hair flew in the wind while Finn showed off how he could pump his legs and keep the swing moving all by himself. Giggles and chatter filled the air.

This sweet memory crossed my mind while doing my morning Bible reading. *1 Thessalonians 1:7-10* says, *"The word has gotten around. Your lives are echoing the Master's word. The news of your faith in God is out. You don't even have to say anything anymore...you're the message!" (MSG)."*

You're the message. I thought of our grandchildren and how just showing up expressed a message of love and how their warm welcome was a message of their love to us. Nothing needed to be said. Just being together expressed our mutual love.

You're the message. I thought of recent tensions in our family due to misunderstanding and lack of compassion. I also thought of our world where the media promotes messages of unrest and dissatisfaction. Racial tensions, politics, Covid, abortion, and a long list of social ills tend to divide us. Many people won't even speak out anymore for fear of nasty things being spewed back at them. Others who do speak up find themselves being shamed for speaking against the negative narrative.

You're the message. How easy it is to throw allegations without understanding, judge when others don't agree with you, or point silent fingers of accusation rather than welcome healthy conversations with boundaries of mutual respect. That sends a message too.

You're the message. Regardless of whether we speak up or stay silent, take a stand or watch and observe, draw a boundary, or raise a flag, wear a mask or not, protest or riot, we send a message. We live in a world where Satan enjoys running mankind through his playground. Whether it's family dynamics or world politics, the enemy has been stirring the pot with the intent to kill, steal, and destroy. God is still in control. Sharing His message is more imperative than ever.

You're the message. I want to be a message of hope and faith in our amazing Savior even when fear is standing at the door. I want to be a message of forgiveness even when the hurts are unbearable. I want to be a message of love, even if it is returned with hate and judgment. I want to be a message of compassion even if others misunderstand.

Will I succeed every time? Absolutely NOT, but at the end of my life, I hope to be remembered as someone who declared God's message so loudly that words weren't needed. You're a message too. What do you want your message to be?

Denise E. Johnson

Muddy Boots

Oh, the joy of being a grandparent. Today it meant going on the kindergarten field trip with our grandson Finn. Little sister Irene had joined us, all too excited to be with big brother for the morning. The sun shimmered on the weekend snow covering, making the temperature just right for a light coat.

Upon arriving at the pumpkin patch, the children were read a wonderful pumpkin story. Then we climbed aboard an open wagon pulled by a tractor and headed out to the corn maze. As we made our way along the muddy road, I questioned whether we'd make it through that much muck. Alas, we arrived at the entrance to the maze and climbed off the wagon.

Our muddy experience had just begun. Tromping through the maze, it wasn't long before untied boots got stuck in the mud and slippery ground landed a few little ones on their bottoms. After only getting lost once, we finally reached the end of the maze with all twelve children and seven adults. As we surveyed our feet, I laughed, noting that almost everyone's boots were twice as large as their actual size, caked with layers of mud.

Thinking back to these enlarged boots, I thought of a man who had recently been called home by Jesus. Pastor Ron Todd had been our family pastor through decades. He and his wife Becky had been a part of our spiritual lives in just about every capacity: He had prayed for me prior to surgeries, attended the funeral of our father, advised us about issues with our children, counseled us in marriage, and prayed over our home. Pastor Ron had also led over seventy mission teams including the three to Ethiopia Kassi and I took. Each trip, Pastor Ron led morning devotions, testimonies, and Sparkle time at the end of the day to share our highlights. He pointed us to Jesus and gave Him glory at every opportunity, all with great energy and enthusiasm. He could outwork men half his age as he clamored across roofs, shaky scaffolding, or scurried around the villages gathering supplies for projects. Pastor Ron had an infectious smile. His long arms equipped him to embrace others in spontaneous bear hugs. He loved Jesus wholeheartedly.

So, what do mud-caked boots have to do with this man? Well, it occurred to me, much like the bulky boots, he was a man who, wherever he went, left a footprint at least twice his foot size. In all he did, more of him and his purpose for life spilled out beyond the task, the project, or the moment. His servanthood for Christ went beyond. Even now, when he is no longer here on earth, he left so much behind, like a mist from a waterfall or a fog that flows through the valley beyond the boundaries of the river. His footprint in life overflowed in ways I'm sure he never imagined.

What a legacy. What an example. What an amazing way to live life that no matter what, it went beyond the moment. Beyond our time here on earth.

Like Pastor Ron, I want to leave a footprint that is way larger than my actual shoe size; one that lingers and overflows into generations to come. *Matthew 28:19 says "Therefore, go and make disciples of nations, baptizing them in the name of the Father and the Son and the Holy Spirit," (NIV)* and might I add, if you leave a little mud along the way, that's okay too.

Denise E. Johnson

Don't Forget Me

I was ready for a quiet evening at home with my husband. We decided to watch a movie and although we'd watched it before, we chose Abraham Lincoln by Steven Spielberg. It really is a must see for everyone. Spoiler alert: I am about to share some thoughts about it.

President Lincoln knew slavery was wrong. In his effort to abolish it, he authorized deals to be brokered, bribes to be paid, whatever it took to get the votes from the opposition. Others tried to convince him the timing was bad or that it couldn't be done, but he wouldn't be swayed. The President remained adamant it had to happen at that moment in time. After exhausting every avenue, he scheduled the vote. Then he prayed fervently and encouraged others to do the same.

On the day of the vote, tensions were high. There weren't enough confirmed votes. As I watched the climax of the movie, even knowing the outcome, I held my breath. One by one the votes were voiced. Then when all seemed lost, two Democratic leaders dramatically crossed party lines and sided with the President. Fellow politicians were outraged. Threats and anger erupted, but it was over. Slavery had been abolished. What courageous men.

As I reflected on the movie, I questioned: Was it really the men who were courageous or God's intervention that gave them the courage? Could it be said they HEARD and obeyed God over the shouts of men?

Watching the movie created sentiment and inspiration. I remember the sense of finality I felt when my doctor told me at the age of thirty-five, I needed a hysterectomy. No more children, such deep grief for the children I'd hoped to have, but now wouldn't. Then God gave us two more children through adoption. Similar unexpected outcomes fill the pages of the Bible. Abraham and Sarah were given their very late-in-life, impossible gift of Isaac. The Israelites, standing at the Red Sea, were given a rescue plan right through the Red Sea when all they could see were the Egyptian chariots pursuing them. How easy it is for us as humans to come to a foregone conclusion without considering what God might do instead. It's almost as if I can picture God waving his hand in the air to get our attention, shouting, "Hey, what about me? Did you forget what I can do?"

Today we stand at another pivotal point in our country's history when votes have the potential of changing our country significantly. God will use courageous men to right wrongs, but we need to be diligent in praying. To continue to look for His plan even when human comprehension has sealed the deal. As we wait upon this final lap in the conclusion of an already torturous election season, I want to live with the expectation of what God will do. I want to be the Israelite who focused on the raging sea knowing God can do anything, not the one watching the dust cloud rise in the distance as the chariots approached.

God isn't done yet. That's why we're still here. Commit to pray for our leaders so they will hear and act on God's will. Pray God will once again save our nation from the sins of abortion and rebellion, just like he saved our nation from the sin of slavery. No matter how things appear, don't forget to factor in God. He's still working out the finale and His endings are amazing.

Mark 10:27: "Jesus looked at them and said, 'With man it is impossible, but not with God. For all things are possible with God." (NIV).

Denise E. Johnson

Heavenly Messages

Anniversaries always carry such weight of emotion, especially that first one. The weeks and days leading up to it are filled with thoughts of what we were doing the previous year, whether the final preparations for a wedding, birthing pains, or in my case, helping Mom live out her final days. The first anniversary of her passing was a few days away. The whole month had been filled with memories that seem too fresh to have truly been a year ago. Tears often welled over the slightest recollection. Imagine my joy when my sister Colleen mentioned she would be coming through town. Sister time always made life better, especially since it would give us time to process and reflect on memories of Mom.

In typical fashion, when Colleen left home, I received a message letting me know she was heading down the road. Not so typical was a phone call while enroute, so when I saw her call coming in, a knot of worry hit me. As I answered, she greeted me with cheer. "Hey, do you have a minute to chat?"

"Sure." I wondered what couldn't wait until she arrived.

Then she explained: "My new car seems to be struggling to sync my text messages. Occasionally I get some random text message. Last week I got a message from you, but when I looked at my phone, I realized it was an old message. It's so weird. Anyway, I've been driving along, and I got a rather startling text message." She paused before finishing her sentence, "From Mom."

"Are you kidding? What did it say?"

"Looking forward to seeing you."

A gasp was followed by nervous laughter and then tears. It felt a bit eerie and yet tender, especially with the timing of it. I then added, "I hope you won't be seeing her before me, since we're supposed to be meeting in an hour, here on earth!" We chatted a bit more and then hung up.

Thankfully, right on schedule, Colleen arrived for a quick lunch and then headed back down the road. Later that afternoon, just before she reached her destination, Colleen called again. She'd just received another message from Mom. This time the text mentioned how much Mom enjoyed their visit, then added she'd been pleased with her morning raspberry harvest.

With the two texts, one could almost imagine that between the, "looking forward to seeing you" and "I so enjoyed your visit", she actually joined us for lunch. Perhaps she had, especially since in the weeks before Mom departed for glory, Colleen suggested Mom join her for lunch sometime. Mom had certainly been a part of our conversation many times that day.

Can I just say, "Wow, God!" The heavenly messages (that had originally been sent fifteen months prior) were a sweet reminder of our mom and how much she treasured relationships. Her get-togethers with friends, trips to be a part of her grandchildren's lives, baking cookies for the neighbors, letters and calls to encourage and stay up to date. Through her example, we learned the value of loving others while growing and maintaining relationships. Could there be anything more important to pass along, especially when the most significant relationship we can have is with our Lord Jesus Christ.

How we miss Mom, but what a tender gift from God. I know she's looking forward to seeing us just as much as we are looking forward to seeing her. What a visit it will be: catching up with her and other loved ones, seeing Jesus face to face, walking the streets of gold, hearing the heavenly choirs, and sitting at the banquet table (oh dear God, I hope there's chocolate).

One thing is certain, when Colleen and I get there, we're heading for the raspberry patch. We're pretty sure that's where we'll find Mom, going about the Lord's work while gathering supplies to make something special for those she loves.

Denise E. Johnson

Building a Family

Written for the love of my life, my husband Ron, as a reminder of our journey over the past years as we were building a family.

We were struggling to have children and buried our first two.
We were betrayed by loved ones and embraced by strangers.
We were hearing words like cancer and wondering what was ahead.
We were pacing in the hallway waiting for the doctor's report.
We were having play dates, birthday parties, and playing board games.
And attending funerals, weddings, and socializing with friends.
We were building a family.

We were running a business and working our jobs, downsized and struggling to make ends meet.
We were planning vacations and savoring it through our children's eyes.
We were fostering children while praying we could adopt them.
We were attending church, Good News Bears, and volunteering too.
We were pacing the floors when it was way past curfew.
And sometimes we cried in the shower to hide the pains of the journey.
We were building a family.

We were helping our grandparents, parents, and relatives with their needs.
We were kissing owwies, wiping bloody noses, and cleaning up puke.
We were tickling our toddlers and chasing away bad dreams.
We were cooling their fevers and rocking them to sleep.
We were exhausted, worn out, and proud all at the same moment.
And, at times, we were simply trying to keep our marriage together.
Yes, we were building a family.

We were wrapping birthday presents and arranging Christmas surprises.
We were comforting our children when they were sad.
We were cheering from the sidelines during games and swim meets.
We were clutching the dashboard when we taught them to drive.
We held back tears when we kissed them goodbye, whether off to kindergarten or the Navy, parting was hard.
We were reminding them they were smart and strong.
And teaching them to say thank you and to mind their manners.
We were building a family.

We were racing to the emergency room, fearing the worst.
We were sending them to camp and going along to chaperone.
We were reminding them to work hard, be kind, and serve others.
We were reading bedtime stories, watching a movie, or talking about life.
We were raising funds for Africa, class trips, and extracurricular activities,
And planning graduation parties, weddings, and showers.
We were building a family.

We were taking walks, bike rides, and 4-wheeling in the hills.
We were feeding them Jello and shakes when the wisdom teeth came out.
We were talking to police when a car accident occurred or heaven forbid, 911 got accidently called.
We were chasing off bad friends and encouraging the good.
We were planning and preparing so they could reach their own dreams.
We were eeking out date time with each other or one of our kids.
And we argued and fought because what we had was worth fighting for.
We were building a family.

We took road trips and plane rides so they could have new experiences.
We were loving our pets and crying when it was time for goodbyes.
We were up late at night working on school projects or a term paper.
We were praying for them with hopes for a beautiful future.
We were pushing strollers and driving icy roads to attend sports events.
We were painting the bedrooms, so each room felt like their own.
And when our parents passed, we made sure they didn't die alone.
We were building a family, but it was more than that. We were building our legacy.

The journey of building takes on many forms.
And there comes a time when you reap your reward.
For sometimes in the effort of building your life
Pieces get lost and need to be restored.
So here we are darling, looking back on our life.
It wasn't perfect nor without fault.
Yet, nothing was missing, not much to regret.
For we lived our lives fully, without holding back.
We built our family.

Awe God

I'm so proud of us honey for with our faith, we did it together
Surviving and thriving what few couples could.
Will our children ever know how much we love them?
The struggles and trials we hid from their lives.
The joy of our miraculous five and now precious grandchildren
They are our whole world. **This family we built.**

As we focus on our next chapter of life.
Creating new memories with hopes they won't fade.
I'll have to admit, I'm a bit selfish of us,
For this is our time to learn more about us.
To rekindle our love and grow in our walk with God.
To understand each other better from this season in time.
And enjoy every moment of our life's work,
Because our treasure is in **the family we built.**

Denise E. Johnson

The Bridge

January 6, 2021: The chaos at the US Capitol and the drama that played out in the media weighed heavy on my heart. I wanted to curl up in my chair and cry or pray. Real life beckoned when my daughter called to ask for help transporting my ten-year-old granddaughter Kyrstan to swimming. I wanted to say no as fatigue and discouragement zapped me of energy, but I could certainly help her in this small way.

    I headed down the familiar road to her house, the one we lived in for seventeen years before she and her husband purchased it from us. Driving over the bridge that goes over the interstate, I noticed a teenage girl on the side of the road. She looked upset, but I'd driven past her by the time it registered what I'd seen. Since the bridge is narrow, I went to the end of the road and then circled back to the bridge. Sight is limited so until I crested the bridge, I couldn't see her. Pulling up next to her, I rolled down my window.

    "Hun, are you okay?" She shook her head no. "Can I help you?" She again indicated no. I glanced in my rearview mirror, worried I could be hit from behind. "I can't leave you here. I promise I'm safe. Please get in the car so I can see how I can help you." She hesitated a moment, then glanced to check for traffic, crossed the road, and climbed into the passenger seat. Before she even buckled herself in, she blurted out, "I was going to jump from the bridge and kill myself."

    I felt like the wind had been knocked out of me as I struggled with what to say. Tears filled my eyes and I reached to touch her while pulling my car off to the side of the road, navigating to a safer location. "I'm so glad you didn't," I choked out. I let some silence fill a moment. As I turned the car around, I added, "I need to get my granddaughter and take her to swimming, but after I drop her off, would you go with me for coffee so we can talk?" She agreed.

As we drove the short distance to my daughter's home, she softly wept. When Kyrstan got in the car, she inquired about my passenger, but accepted my "she's a friend" response. Before long, the girls were chatting about games and apps I'd never heard of. As they visited, I learned her name and that she was sixteen. I appreciated Kyrstan who helped break the ice.

After dropping off Kyrstan, my new friend and I went to a coffee shop. She shared that her friend had recently died. I let her vent and cry, then told her I also lost my best friend at about her age. I reminded her that God is always with us and for us. While we sipped on our hot drinks, she made a few calls and soon came up with a plan. An hour later, I dropped her off at a home she assured me was safe while she waited for her uncle to come get her. As I gave her a hug, I handed her my card and peered into her face. "Someday, someone will need you as much as you needed someone tonight. Please be there for them. Don't quit on life." She nodded through her tears as she returned my hug and thanked me.

God deserves all the honor and glory for what happened. I simply did what any decent person would do. Had I remained in my sulking slump due to the January 6th events at the Capitol, I'd have missed out on the most important task God planned for me that day. I am so grateful He used me for that brief moment in that young woman's life. The encounter changed my life and hopefully hers as well. What a powerful reminder that He is always at work. Even on hard days, He has kingdom work for us to do. Sometimes it's just a matter of showing up.

Galatians 6:9, "So let's not allow ourselves to get fatigued doing good. At the right time we will harvest a good crop if we don't give up, or quit." (MSG)

Denise E. Johnson

Rocky Trails

Trudging up the steep mountain trail, my much more athletic sister led the way. While I struggled to keep my footing on the rocky path, Colleen climbed the trail like a sure-footed mountain goat. I had already suggested she go ahead, knowing full well I wouldn't have the fortitude to tackle this mountain like she could. Around halfway up, I could no longer see her. Meanwhile, my shaking knees and trembling legs had reached their limit.

Finding a large rock near the path, I sat to await Colleen's return. By then, hopefully I'd have enough steam to make it back down the mountain with her.

Months later, while reading my Bible, my exhausting mountain climb came to mind. *Luke 18:35-42 (MSG)* shares the story of a blind man sitting beside the road. When he heard Jesus approaching, he called out. Those ahead of Jesus told the man to shut up, but he yelled all the louder. When Jesus heard him, he listened and healed him. The once, and no longer blind man, then followed Jesus, glorifying God. Everyone in the street joined in, shouting praises to God.

What struck me about this passage and thus made me think of the rocky trail was two-fold. First, this blind man sat by the road. He didn't want to be missed. Much like me waiting for my sister to return back down the trail, I didn't want to be left up there by myself. I knew if I stayed close to the trail, she'd see me and drag me off the mountain if needed.

If we want to have an encounter with Jesus, we need to be on the path where Jesus is. That starts with spending time reading our Bibles so we are trained to hear His voice and understand His will and purpose. Otherwise, it can be easy to be dragged off His path by deceptive or false teachings.

The second thought that came to mind is, like the blind man, we have to speak up, even yell if necessary. So many are afraid to speak up out of fear of being belittled. We have a responsibility to speak for what is good and right. Countless soldiers died defending our freedoms, including our freedom to speak freely. We also have a responsibility to speak up for those who can't; children being trafficked, the elderly and infirmed, and the unborn.

Most importantly, we have a responsibility to speak up about the good news of Christ. Even if others disagree or brush us aside, we must respectfully speak up for what honors and glorifies God.

This life isn't an easy journey. In fact, it's a lot like trying to keep up with my agile sister on that rocky path. We might feel breathless, out-of-shape, and exhausted. At times, our knees might even shake, but as long as we stay on the path and speak up, we can be counted in God's great army of warriors. So, on your feet warriors! We've got a mountain to climb for God's glory.

Denise E. Johnson

By My Spirit

I'd recently been turned onto audio books which made great company on my road trips and walks. Although I hadn't finished my last book, I had some credits to use up. One of Lynn Austin's titles caught my attention: "Return to Me." A few weeks later, my dear friend Pam asked if I wanted to participate in a Bible study. I had missed the last year due to life's demands, but I love studying the Word with other women. So, I committed without even asking about the subject of the study.

About the time our Haggai Bible study started, I also began listening to my new book. I realized both the Bible study and the audiobook were about the Israelites who returned to Jerusalem to rebuild the temple. How fun to study this through two different perspectives.

One morning during my walk, the narrator of my audiobook shared the words of the prophet Zechariah as he proclaimed, *"Not by might nor power, but by my Spirit."* Twenty minutes later I sat to work on my Bible study. As I started through the questions, the study directed me to look up a Scripture in *Zechariah 4:6. "So he said to me, 'This is the word of the Lord to Zerubbabel: Not by might nor by power, but by my Spirit,' says the Lord Almighty." (NIV)* A chill ran down my spine. What were the odds of hearing the exact same Scripture from a book I downloaded months ago, on the same morning I read it in my unplanned Bible study? None, Nada, Zilch.

It was providential, as if God spoke directly to me, "My precious daughter, some things can only be resolved by my Spirit." I sat back into my chair, closed my eyes, and tried to absorb God's very timely message. A personal issue that wrecked my heart immediately came to mind. With all my might, I tried to resolve it. I'd prayed, sought counseling, shed thousands of tears, and lost hours of sleep. I'd written letters, made phone calls, and driven miles. Still, the issue remained, unresolved and hurting like an open wound that wouldn't heal.

A picture came to mind: a child beaten up in the school yard, his lunch stolen in the process. Exhausted from the fight, he withdrew to sit alone on a bench. Then his dad showed up. Immediately the child ran to him. As his father gathered him into his arms, the child's tears dried. His fear dissolved: his confidence had returned. He knew he no longer had to defend himself.

I felt a peace come over me. My Father was here too. As much as I wanted to fix things, it was simply beyond my ability. It would take His Spirit because, like many things where the enemy is at work, spiritual battles can only be won by spiritual forces.

As we observe the forces of evil divide our country and our families, do not lose hope. Sometimes we must put aside our own desires and efforts and simply wait for Him. I don't know about you, but waiting is the hard part because I'd much rather be doing. *"God proves to be good to the man who passionately waits, to the woman who diligently seeks. It's a good thing to quietly hope for help from God." Lamentations 3:25-27 (MSG).*

Even if we could fix the pains of life, it wouldn't have the profound results of God's handiwork. So I wait, seeking and focusing on Him while aching to see His glory. The battle is His. It can only be won by the Holy Spirit. He will be the victor. He is Daddy, Abba Father after all.

Denise E. Johnson

Her Hands

I woke up this morning with stiff joints in my fingers, likely a result of my previous night's sewing project. I squeezed my hands into fists. They would be fine after my shower. My temporary pain made me pause and think of the many things I enjoyed doing with my hands. Typing my blogs, sewing, craft projects, giving my grandchildren backrubs and tickles, massaging my husband's shoulders, or ruffling my son Josh's hair. What can I say, he has great hair!

As I thought of all the things I enjoy because of my hands, I couldn't help but think of my mother, who used her hands to teach me so much. She gave us childhood backrubs, taught us to sew, showed us how to bake a cake, peel potatoes, cut carrots, plant seeds, and husk corn. Mom's hands had combed my hair and spanked my bottom. Her hands created beautiful music. I remember many evenings gathered around the piano as Mom or Colleen played and we all sang. Mom would harmonize her alto voice with my soprano. Our mini-concerts always ended with the song: "God Be with You till We Meet Again."

Today would have been Mom's eighty-fifth birthday. Trust me, there would have been an all-out party. Mom loved social events. Memories of her 80th birthday party are fresh in my mind, the birthday cake shaped like a sewing machine, the songs sang to her by her grandchildren, the guests who came to celebrate her. I'm so glad we put the party together. We had so much fun. We never imagined it would be one of her last birthdays here with us on earth.

In Mom's final weeks, massaging her hands helped her to relax. Holding them assured her we were there, and she wasn't alone. As we prayed together with our hands all joined together, she expressed love and concern for each of her grandchildren and children. When the cancer spread, her hands swelled with fluid. Although they no longer looked quite like her hands, when she extended them to us, they communicated her love.

I'm so grateful for Mom's hands that taught me how to use my hands to work, play, and serve others. Because of her example and legacy, there is one thing I'm certain of. She is still using her hands to love and serve our Lord. For as our familiar childhood song reminds us, God is indeed with Mom and with us, until we meet again. Happy Birthday Mom.

""Look! Look! God has moved into the neighborhood, making his home with men and women! They're his people, He's their God. He'll wipe every tear from their eyes. Death is gone for good—tears gone, crying gone, pain gone—all the first order of things gone." Revelations. 21:3-4 (MSG).

"I thank God every time I remember you…being confident of this, that he who began a good work in your will carry it on to completion until the day of Christ Jesus." Philippians 1:3-6 (NIV).

Denise E. Johnson

The Remnant

Full disclosure: I love to save remnants, those little pieces of fabric that aren't large enough for the main project, but just large enough for something smaller. I'm pretty sure I got this habit from my mom. Probably the only difference between her pile of remnants and mine is, her pile could fill a room, while mine is limited to a single container. When they overflow the container, it's time to find a use for them. My latest project has been making children's frog-shaped pillows.

Remnants can be meaningless scraps that are tossed away or the beginnings of something greater. In Biblical terms it references what is left of a population after a catastrophe. When Noah and his family boarded the ark, they became the remnant of the human race. When the Jews were taken captive, a remnant was always left, therefore the Jews were never extinguished. In the worst of times, God always recognized and preserved a small population who were faithful to His truths.

Imagine being Noah as he built the ark. Some scholars estimate it took him around seventy years. I wonder how many times Noah felt alone, confused, or unsure as the 25,000+ days passed; or how often he heard disparaging words, even from people who loved him. To have even completed the task, his faith in God had to have a stick-to-it-ness like most of us can't even imagine. Because of it, Noah and his family were saved as God's remnant to repopulate the earth.

Today we are assaulted with agendas and propaganda that leave us feeling confused, unsure, and sometimes alone. The only certainty we have is God's Word, which provides clear direction and guidance.

We are all sinners. We all fail, myself included. Except for the blood of Christ, we'd all be lost. In the chaos of this life, it is easy to become deceived, and forget it is our faith in God and His Word that sets us apart. We must be willing to stand on God's Word, not man's opinion. We must stand for His truths by protecting the unborn and defending the sacredness of marriage. We must be prepared to call out sin with grace, even if it is perceived as intolerant. It's about honoring God's Word, which stands way above public opinion and political agendas.

There is always a remnant. We can choose to be a useless scrap or a remnant of loyalty, shaped by His hands, disciplined by His Holy Spirit, and useful for His purposes. I want to be counted as a Noah who remained devoted to God's Word, even in the face of criticism and unpopular opinion.

God's Word has never changed. His love has never changed. His sacrifice has never changed. He is looking for the Noahs of this generation who are loyal to Him and His Word so that humanity will once again seek Him, the Holy One.

"Then the LORD said to Noah, 'Go into the ark, you and all your household, for I have seen that you are righteous before me in this generation." Genesis 7:1 (ESV).

Denise E. Johnson

The Shepherd

It's all my sister's fault. She wanted to raise lambs for 4-H and before we knew it, Dad had a herd of sheep. Adorable as they are, they are followers and will blindly follow one another, even when there is danger. They are rather helpless too. If they get stuck on their backs, they will die that way unless someone helps right them. They don't seem to have a fight to survive. I remember one bitter cold night during lambing season, a set of twins couldn't seem to get hooked up to their mama for milk. Colleen and I were out in the barn in the middle of the night, trying to get them to latch onto their mama. Her warm milk quickly turned ice cold, numbing our fingers. We were working harder than the lambs, trying to get milk in their tummies.

    I also remember a night waking up to the sound of dogs in the pasture. I could hear the sheep's pounding feet as they ran and their frantic bleating, as well as the growling and panting of dogs in the chase. I called out to Dad. Breathless with adrenaline, I stammered, "Dogs!" He shot out of bed before I'd even completed the word.

    The Bible is full of stories about sheep and shepherds. Because of my childhood experiences, the numerous analogies are very relatable. Like sheep, we sometimes follow along because it's easier than going against the flow. We can be blind to life's dangers and vulnerable to missteps, especially if we are listening to the wrong people. We need a protector, just like the sheep did in the middle of the night when I called out to Dad.

    Fortunately, we have a protector. Jesus is our protector, our helper to guide our steps, fill our minds with wisdom, and give us discernment. We are important to Him, but we can only hear Him if we are listening for His voice. It's a noisy world and recently, it's been filled with so much fear. To drown it out and hear Him, we need to be intentional about our time with Him, setting our eyes on our shepherd while turning our ears off to agendas that promote fear.

Jeremiah 23:1-4 states: "Doom to the shepherd-leaders who butcher and scatter my sheep!" GOD's Decree. 'So here is what I, GOD, Israel's God, say to the shepherd-leaders who misled my people: You've scattered my sheep. You've driven them off. You haven't kept your eye on them. Well, let me tell you, I'm keeping my eye on you, keeping track of your criminal behavior. I'll take over and gather what's left of my sheep, gather them in from all the lands where I've driven them. I'll bring them back where they belong, and they'll recover and flourish. I'll set shepherd-leaders over them who will take good care of them. They won't live in fear or panic anymore. All the lost sheep rounded up!" (MSG).

We don't know what is around the corner, what tomorrow will bring, or even what is ahead in the next hour, but we know we have a good Shepherd. He doesn't need to be awakened in the night to hear our call. He stands ready to gather us back together, so we can recover and flourish. We don't need to live in fear, now or ever! Let's be sure in these uncertain times we are following the One true Shepherd.

Denise E. Johnson

What Lingers

What a weekend we'd had. It had been crazy, full, and exhausting as we babysat our granddaughters, ages three and one. The energy needed to keep up was endless. I might add, we're not thirty anymore! Only hours into our weekend, we'd been through every fun activity in the house. Thank goodness bedtime was soon.

    Our daughter had given us very good instructions on bedtime routines for the baby, Tilly. "Easy" is how she'd put it. "Just say goodnight, wave goodbye and give her the blankie and bottle." Again, I emphasize "easy". Well, that didn't work. Instead, after that routine I rocked Tilly, careful to not make eye contact while stealing a peek until her eyes fluttered shut. When her body made sleepy twitches, I thought I was in the clear. Then came the attempted stealthy move to get her into the crib without waking her. Well, so much for my stealth. Nanny ended up laying on the floor within Tilly's sight, again not making eye contact, until she finally gave up. Note: Nanny might have fallen asleep right there on the floor before Tilly did.

    In my own bed at last, an occasional whimper woke me from a shallow sleep. Morning came too quickly, but with the first sounds of her cry, I opened her bedroom door. She greeted me with a sweet smile and outstretched arms. With her arms looped around my neck, I carried her to the rocker where she laid her head on my chest, and we quietly rocked as she took her time waking up. The scent of a wet diaper reminded me of the next order of business, but only after savoring this precious quiet moment.

    So it went for two days and nights, learning little tricks to keep our darlings happy and entertained. The girls joined me on morning walks, provided an audience while I used the bathroom, and shared the mirror while we brushed our teeth, washed our faces, and patted lotion onto our skin. The giggles, tired tears, happy smiles, and snuggles were treasures.

As our weekend with the girls came to an end, we gathered their things and took them home. Back at our home we picked up the toys, wiped the sticky juice from the floor, and collapsed into our easy chairs. In the quiet, I could still hear their chatter and the pitter patter of their feet on the floor. No, I wasn't losing my mind. It's just my maternal ear had been recalibrated to their sounds that lingered as a sweet memory.

It made me think of my journey with the Lord and how I want His words to linger long after I've spent time with Him. How I want to live out Sunday church beyond the hour, and how desperately I want my life to honor him as noted in *James 1:22 - 25: "Do not merely listen to the word. Do what it says. Anyone who listens to the word but does not do what it says is like someone who looks at his face in a mirror and, after looking at himself, goes away and immediately forgets what he looks like. But whoever looks intently into the perfect law that gives freedom, and continues in it, not forgetting what they have heard, but doing it, they will be blessed in what they do." (NIV)*.

May the sweet fragrance of our Lord, who gave his life for us, linger in our lives beyond the daily moments and into eternity.

Denise E. Johnson

The Comforter

As we parked in our daughter's driveway to join them for the fourth of July celebrations, our three-year-old granddaughter Irene, came rushing out their door. Tears streamed down her face as she ran to me as fast as her legs would carry her. As she covered the nearly fifty feet, she sobbed over and over, "Nanny, Nanny." Reaching for her, I scooped her up in my arms and held her close. "Oh honey, what is the matter?"

Too upset for words, she pushed out her lower lip. The red and swollen lip said it all. She had taken a fall and wanted me to comfort her and make her feel better. Or at the very least, get as much mileage out of the owwie as possible.

As the mother of now grown children, it had been some time since I'd felt needed to comfort my children's owwies. Holding little Irene, a sense of warmth spread through my heart. Her crisis seemed to fill a void I hadn't realized was there; the need to comfort my loved ones. I fussed over her and when we hugged again, I told her it would be okay. Soon the tears dried and we were onto more fun things.

Later in the evening, as I got ready for bed, I reflected on that sweet moment when all Irene wanted was to tell her Nanny about her owwie. It caused me to think of my Lord and Savior, and I wondered if perhaps He felt the same; watching us go about our lives, sorting through the painful, difficult moments, and waiting for us to run to Him to share our hurts. In our adult independence, sometimes we don't pause to recognize our comforter is right there.

"Come to me, all you who are weary and burdened, and I will give you rest. Take my yoke upon you and learn from me, for I

am gentle and humble in heart, and you will find rest for your souls. For my yoke is easy and my burden is light." Matthew 11:28-30 (NIV).

In this journey of life, at some time or another, we all need to be comforted. I also think we were built to comfort others because doing so creates unique connections.

What a blessing to comfort my granddaughter and connect in that tender way. I suspect God takes great delight in pouring out His comforting love as well. He awaits us with open arms, ready to scoop us up, to soothe our hurts, and remind us everything will be okay. As I go about my days, I want to be more intentional about giving my Creator the delight of being my Comforter.

Denise E. Johnson

Mom's Christmas Gift

The older woman stood ahead of me in the grocery store line. She looked tired. Her gray hair and wrinkled face revealed her more advanced age. It made me think of Mom. I thought of her a lot lately since it was Christmas time, Mom's favorite holiday. Last year just before Christmas, God called her home to glory. This year, despite the number of things I'd thought to buy her for Christmas, there was no need.

My eyes wandered to the conveyor belt that contained a modest selection of groceries. Like getting a poke in the ribs, God prompted me to buy a gift for Mom this year. Stepping forward, I placed my hand on the woman's shoulder. She jumped a bit, startled by my touch. Due to Covid, there hadn't been much touching. I told her I wanted to buy her groceries and without waiting for a response, slipped my credit card in the machine. She couldn't seem to form words, but finally stammered, "I have the money."

"I'm sure you do," I replied. "Use it to enjoy the holidays for another purpose." She tried to talk me out of it, but I insisted. With firm finality I stated, "I don't get to buy my mother a gift this year. Let this be my gift to her." With that, she seemed out of responses as tears filled her eyes. Maybe they were my tears, but either way, we both became a blurry mess.

After her groceries were bagged, she couldn't seem to leave, struggling with what to say. Once she'd gathered herself, she asked, "What is your name, and would you please give me your address or phone number so my husband can thank you too."

"It's not necessary. I've been adequately thanked. Just be blessed with the love of Christ as I have been. Have a Merry

Christmas." With another stammered thank you, she gathered her grocery bags, gave me a hug, Covid and all, and departed.

    The void left due to Mom's absence seemed to lift. Although I didn't get to deliver a gift to Mom this Christmas, I'm pretty sure she received it. Merry Christmas Mom. Thank you for teaching me the joy of serving and giving to others.

Denise E. Johnson

The Wrong Porch

When we departed from the rental home after our family gathering, we didn't realize my ten-year-old granddaughter's childhood bunny had been left on the couch. We were hours away before Leena, with great concern, noted her bunny wasn't with us. Her mother gave it to her prior to deploying overseas eight years earlier, so it wasn't just another bunny. It was a very special one.

As we pulled into the gas station, we searched the car one more time. I then sent a frantic text to the homeowner of the rental. Minutes later, a reply indicated the bunny had been located. They would pop it in the mail the next week. Tremendous relief swept over all of us, knowing it would only be a matter of time before there could be a reunion.

The days went by, and no package arrived. I made another call, only to learn it hadn't been sent yet. Again, relief. At least it hadn't been lost in the mail. This time I left instructions to please include a tracking number. Although it was irreplaceable, the number would at least assure it could be located.

Still, it didn't arrive. When I looked up the tracking number, it indicated it had been left on the doorstep, three days ago! Grief swept over all of us, knowing the devastation Leena would feel if her bunny had been stolen or lost. My daughter-in-law began searching anywhere it might have gotten left, and checked the neighbor's security camera. Meanwhile I prayed.

Not long after, the phone rang. Seeing my daughter-in-law's phone number, my hopes were lifted. She sounded breathless as she explained she'd gone to the next street over, which had the same house number and sure enough, the box sat on the porch, as if waiting to be claimed. Sorrow turned into celebration as she took the box home and presented it to Leena, who was beyond joyous to have her long-lost bunny.

As I praised God for His miracle, I thought of how excited Leena must be. What a testament of God's faithfulness to a little girl to have found her most precious bunny. Only God could have kept a lost bunny safe on the wrong porch for three days. What a perfect opportunity for Leena to understand how extraordinarily happy God is when one of His lost children returns to Him.

In life, sometimes we find ourselves lost or on the "wrong porch". We think we're married to the wrong person, have the wrong job, or the wrong boss. Or we might find, through a series of poor choices, we are simply in the wrong place, much like the prodigal son after taking his inheritance and blowing it. When the prodigal realized he was in the wrong place, he returned to his father, ready to be his slave. Instead, his father welcomed him back as his son. *Luke 15:24: "For this my son was dead, and is alive again; he was lost, and is found. And they began to celebrate." (ESV).*

No matter how wrong things are in life, one thing is always right: God! He always knows where we are. We are His precious treasure, even more than a lost bunny is to a heartbroken child. No matter how "wrong" things are, God can make it right, and no matter how long or how far we've gone from Him, He is ready to welcome us home and celebrate when we return to Him.

Denise E. Johnson

He Wins

As I struggled to remain on my feet, I grabbed for the curtain of the temporary triage station, grasping for something solid to keep me upright. Nurses grabbed my arms and quickly plopped me into a wheelchair. I then realized I was much sicker than I thought as the six-day 103.8 temperature ravaged my strength.

After a gentle ride across the street to the emergency room, the medical team started an IV, then blood work and a CT scan. I sent a quick text to my Bible study leader Pam, asking for prayers. As the diagnosis came, Covid pneumonia, I did my best to jot notes into my phone as doctors detailed the protocol, talking to me as if I was actually coherent. Remdesivir came up. It pricked my mind. I think that's a no, but I couldn't remember. Moments later, without prompting, Pam texted me and confirmed. "Don't take Remdesivir." When the next attendee came into the room, I asked her to take it off my list of medications.

Hours of waiting finally netted a hospital room. The next forty-eight hours were a blur of sleep and an occasional stagger to the bathroom, clutching walls to avoid falling. I knew I had no choice but to advocate for myself. No one else could be there to help. I also needed to advocate for Ron, who had a fever as well. When I asked questions about my care, it was for him too. His illness had started about a week after mine and I couldn't let him get this sick. I needed to get out of here so I could get eyes on him.

After two nights in the hospital, I demanded to be released. With the necessary medications, I would recover better at home. At five pm, I walked out the hospital door with a temporary oxygen tank. Josh met me at the door and drove me home. When I saw Ron,

I broke into sobs. He was so sick. I needed to be here. Just like every other crisis in life, we needed each other.

Oxygen was brought to our home for my ongoing care. The technician gave instructions from the door since we were quarantined, but I didn't need them. This was all too familiar since I helped my mom with her oxygen needs during her final weeks, less than two years ago.

Settling into my recliner, the swishing sounds of the oxygen concentrator swept me back into the past, refreshing the grief of Mom's passing. At that moment, can I admit? I just wanted my mommy. I needed her embrace, her reminder that everything was going to be okay.

In the days of recovery that followed, my emotions were wild. One moment I felt white hot mad, thinking of all who suffered from Covid. The next minute, I was overcome with tears of gratitude for all the blessings from God; my friends who were praying, Ron, who recovered quickly due to monoclonal antibodies, and our children, who were attentive to our needs. Grief mixed in it all as the swish, swish of the oxygen condenser continued.

I was so tired, but weren't we all? After a year of Covid, we were tired of watching evil sweep across our beautiful country. Tired of the Covid panic and the suffering from misinformation and fear mongering, of being told what we could do, what rights we had, and who we could be with. We all just wanted to hug our neighbors and not be judged for our own personal choices. Why did we even have to discuss them? What made others think they had a right to judge? Just stay in your own lane!

There it was again, hostile anger. Plain ole' mad and it wasn't going to help me get better. So, I did what I always should do. I turned to God and prayed. I surrendered once again to His will and purpose. I begged him to give me His full heart of compassion and to help me be the person He intended me to be. I needed His strength to continue the battle, especially the one raging in my mind.

Then He reminded me. "My daughter, my precious daughter. I win. I always win. I have overcome the world. I know everything you are struggling with and guess what? I am bigger. All these battles belong to me and I win." It felt like receiving a much-needed embrace from my mama in heaven.

So, my sweet friends, I want to encourage and remind you. No matter how tired you are, or the fight you're facing, as long as you keep your eyes on Christ and commit yourself to His calling and purpose, everything is going to be okay, because HE ALWAYS WINS.

John 16:33 "I have told you these things, so that in me you may have peace. In this world you will have trouble. But take heart! I have overcome the world." (NIV).

Just Another Stat

Yep, the one statistic I hadn't wanted to contribute to was the Covid stats. Yet here I was, testing positive. After being admitted to the hospital, I felt the loneliness of isolation, especially after my phone died. Aren't we just helpless without our phones? My goodness. In the quiet, I took some time to reflect. Life's experiences are meant to teach us, and I was determined to take something away from this experience. Here's what I learned:

1) Choices have consequences. I chose not to be vaccinated and although this is the worst illness I've ever endured, I stand by my choice. Even God gave us choice, rather than forcing His will upon us. Why should any entity have the right to take mine or yours away? I am now fully immunized by God's design with natural antibodies which are way more effective than the vaccine. I gratefully count myself among the 99.95% Covid survivors.

2) In this era, we must be our own advocates. Sometimes, that means asking for help. I wish I'd gone in to get checked sooner. There are solutions and medications to help us. Ask for help. There is nothing heroic about being sick longer than necessary.

3) There's always some give and take. Fortunately, I had been researching this virus prior to my own crisis, so when I found myself listening to the protocols for treatment, I was prepared to make my own decisions. When hospital staff asked me about Remdesivir and intubation, I refused. As far as the uncomfortable mesh hospital underwear, well, they are temporary. Just go with them.

4) No matter how sick you are, if God's not done with you, you're going to live to see another day. I began seeking His purpose for the next portion of my life. I strongly felt God giving me a new task, so I focused on that, not the illness. It helped me look forward with expectation.
5) Do things that feel good; wash your face, put on lotion, pray and quote Scripture, and enjoy the quiet. I realized I needed more quiet space in my life. Doing things that made me feel good gave me energy to advocate for myself when I felt so awful.
6) Laughter is great medicine. Now that you own the remote control (some of us don't at home...ha), find something funny to watch on TV. I found the Golden Girls on the Hallmark channel. It felt so good to just laugh.
7) Keep things in perspective. Yes, Covid is a killer, just like cancer, heart disease, and diabetes, but death is a part of life. We cannot allow any illness or setback to dictate our lives. If we do, we can lose sight of why we are living. I was reminded to not waste valuable time over pettiness or divisive issues. Instead, focus on Christ and His purpose, because there will always be people who want to suck us dry with their negativity. God is counting on us to stand for Him and His children, no matter who disagrees, including standing for freedoms to make our own health care decisions.
8) Remember, we are never just another statistic to our Heavenly Father. *Matthew 10:30–31 states: "And even the very hairs on your head are numbered. So don't be afraid; you are worth more than many sparrows." (NIV).* God deemed the world incomplete without each of us. No matter what we face, even in an isolated Covid hospital room, we are never alone and need not be afraid.

So?

During my quiet time with the Lord this morning, I read Moses' account when God called him to go back to Egypt and free the Israelites. I couldn't help but smile as I read Moses' excuses. "They won't believe me or listen to me" and "I can't speak well." Sounds familiar, right? I've used those myself on a few occasions. Let's face it, we humans are really good at making excuses, especially if we don't want to get out of a nice warm bed to do something that's not fun, like shoveling the winter snow off the driveway.

This was important though. God wanted the Israelites to be free. He chose Moses to help bring about that freedom; a foreshadowing of Christ coming to give us freedom from our sins.

Sometimes we don't give freedom its full credit, especially since most Americans have never known anything but freedom. Unlike many countries, we can choose our profession, whether we'll have children and how many, and where we will shop. How often do we squander our freedoms? We have the freedom to forgive and live in peace, or stir the pot of divisiveness. We have the freedom to attend church, or sleep in; to encourage others, or ignore them; read our Bibles, or watch TV. We have the freedom to follow Christ, or be distracted by work or hobbies. Can we just admit, we're really good at making excuses and in doing so, can squander our freedoms.

Scripture in *Exodus 5:1 says: "Free my people (or let my people go in other translations) so they can hold a festival for me in the wilderness." (MSG)*

In Exodus 6:10-11: "God said to Moses, 'Go and speak to Pharaoh king of Egypt so that he will release the Israelites from his land." (MSG).

Smack dab in the middle of both these verses is an important word: SO. The instruction ahead of the SO was meant for a specific purpose. Free the people SO they could worship. Talk to Pharoah SO there is freedom.

There is a "SO" in our lives too. Do we use our freedoms SO our lives are comfortable? Or do we use our freedoms SO God can use us to influence the next generation, to further his kingdom, and spread His good news? If we let anything, whether it be excuses, fear, insecurity, or distrust keep us from doing the "SO" in our lives, we could miss the reason we're here. Whatever "SO" we're called to fulfill, God will equip us, hopefully with something other than a staff that turns into a snake. That makes me shudder.

"SO" is such an itty-bitty word, but it has the power to change the trajectory of lives, including our own. It also has the power to free people from bad habits and choices, and move forward in new directions. So? What are you letting hold you back from the "SO" that God has made you to do?

The Shorter Road

Have you ever looked back on a season of life and thought, "Wow, that sure seemed harder than it should have been?" Or, "If only I'd known, I would have done that differently."

Today I stumbled upon a passage in *Exodus 13:17 18*. It describes the Israelites leaving Egypt. *"But God didn't lead them by the road through the land of Philistines, which was the shortest route...but led them on the wilderness road, looping around to the Red Sea." (MSG).*

There was a shorter road and yet, that's not the one God chose. Instead, he put them on the wilderness road toward the Red Sea. If He hadn't, they would have missed the Red Sea. In fact, we all would have missed the Red Sea. Can you imagine telling Bible stories without being able to share the story of the Red Sea? It's one of the BIG moments in the Bible when we all get to see the intentional purpose of God, His saving grace, and His sea-parting, mountain-moving power.

Reading this made me pause and reflect. Were there times when He directed me to the longer route? I thought of when our business partner embezzled tens of thousands of dollars. We ended up in court with hopes of getting our investment returned, but instead, the judge gave us the business. That turned into seven years of running a restaurant, something we never planned. However, the longer road led to meeting amazing people and learning new skills. Whoever thought I'd learn to roll sushi? Then I thought about life itself, how God allowed our daughter, Amy Colleen, to take the shorter route to heaven when she was stillborn, while my mother traveled the longer route with eighty-three vibrant years, full of experiences and rich with relationships.

I thought of our country. It is on a wilderness road right now as moral decay accelerates, babies continue to be murdered, and violence robs innocence. We find ourselves praying God will right the wrongs we human beings have allowed to pervade our nation. We want the short route, but perhaps we need the longer road to appreciate what we have, to value the freedoms we've taken for granted, and to learn to stand on our own feet. Although the shorter road might seem better, God often uses the wilderness roads to teach us the most important lessons about ourselves and Him.

If we find ourselves on a long wilderness road, remember that in every step, God is there. He is anxious for us to seek His direction and wisdom, but we can't just stand there, waiting for something to happen. We have to start walking. That's when the journey begins. Once we round the bend, who knows what Red Sea moment might be waiting for us too. One thing is for sure: I don't want to miss it by taking the short road.

Listen Up

As I've become older, I've been able to look back at my life and understand why God allowed certain things to happen. It's like watching a puzzle come together and seeing how each piece equipped me for His calling and purpose for my life.

For me, part of my calling has been child welfare advocacy and reform. God used my love for children to catapult me smack dab into the middle of some of the most heart-wrenching circumstances. As difficult as it is, there is great satisfaction and joy in knowing I'm doing what he assigned me to do, at least for this season.

I must admit though, recently this assignment has felt like a heavy burden. New families call weekly, each one requiring a great deal of compassion, energy, and advocacy. Besides helping families, there is so much research to do, conversations to have with fellow advocates, phone calls to educate and bring along support, leaders to identify who will help, and meetings to organize and attend. My energy has been waning. There just wasn't enough of me to go around, especially when I throw in six precious grandchildren, three adult children, a husband, a house, and some ongoing health issues.

It had been a long day so as I hit SEND on my last email, I pushed away from my computer, ready to take a break. As I did, my eyes landed on my Bible. I felt a longing, so I opened it to where I'd left off and read Exodus 18. A smile came across my face as I realized God had once again aligned His Word directly over my current circumstances.

Exodus 18:17-24 shares the story of Jethro, father-in-law to Moses. As Jethro watched Moses work, Jethro said, *"This is no way to go about it. You'll burn out, and the people right along with you.*

This is way too much for you; you can't do this alone. Now listen to me." Jethro encouraged Moses to identify leaders to help with the work and finished with: *"If you handle the work this way, you'll have the strength to carry out whatever God commands you, and the people will flourish also. Moses listened to the counsel of his father-in-law and did everything he said." (MSG).*

It couldn't have been clearer. I knew the time had come to start shifting some things in life so my calling didn't have such a staggering weight. It was time to listen and make whatever changes God might have me make.

In our hurry scurry society, we often take on more than we should. Sometimes we don't listen to the counsel of others. Pride or fatigue can keep us propped in a place or mindset that needs to be released. Yet, even Moses, a man of God, needed counsel and was wise enough to listen and respond.

Perhaps we have a Jethro in our lives who cares enough to speak wisdom over us. If so, are we humbling ourselves to hear their words of wisdom? If we don't have a Jethro, we still have the Scriptures that are as relevant today as when they were written. We need to be people who listen to the advice of those who honor the Word of God and follow Him. For without wise counsel, we, nor the people around us, can flourish.

The Most Wonderful Time of the Year?

Christmas is my favorite time of the year. I love the decorations, the music, and the movies that make me grab a tissue. I love baking goodies I shouldn't eat, and gathering with loved ones. I love the frenzy in the air as the community comes together to purchase Toys for Tots and fill the needs on the Angel Tree. I am in awe as I see the generosity of so many who pour into the lives of those who have less.

Christmas is also a bit painful for me. Now that my children are grown and live in other communities, I feel the winds of change, knowing we won't be together every year as we have in the past. I long for the days when we were all gathered together in the same home. With those feelings, I can't help but think of the foster children in our community.

Many don't have recollections of being a family, while others simply want their own families back. Some wonder if this will be their last foster home, or if before the year is over, they will have to move again. Still others simply want to belong and feel wanted.

In the past week, I met a grandmother who hasn't seen her grandson in over four months because he's in foster care. I visited with a struggling single mom who will be alone for Christmas because her children are in foster care. I visited with another mom who has been fostering a baby boy for a year. She's worried because she has no idea what is going to happen to him. He'd been delivered to their home when he was only days old. No one had been in touch with her since.

Whether it's foster children, foster parents, or biological parents, their lives are in limbo. Even case workers struggle with the magnitude of cases they must handle as they try to take on the holidays for their own families, as well as the children they serve. I am so grateful for the many people who look out for children who are neglected or abused, but state agencies and temporary foster placements can never replace family. Children need permanent, safe, loving families.

As we close out another year, I would like to send out an appeal on behalf of the thousands of children and families involved in foster care. Let's work harder to keep families together by coming alongside them in their time of need. Let's connect with foster families and help them carry the load of additional children in their families. Let's find solutions to the crisis so next year, instead of needing thousands of toys for foster children, we only need several hundred. We can all do just a little more, considering how blessed we are as a nation and community. No matter where one is in the foster care system, the holidays can be especially painful.

Deuteronomy 24:19: "When you reap your harvest in your field and forget a sheaf in the field, you shall not go back to get it. It shall be for the sojourner, the fatherless, and the widow, that the LORD your God may bless you in all the work of your hands." (ESV).

In this nation of abundance, most of us don't need all that we have. Let's decide to use our resources to bless others instead of spoiling ourselves.

The Fun One

I don't think there is anything that makes heaven feel closer than when we must send off one of our own. My big brother Dave made his journey in the early morning hours of August 11, 2022; gone from his pain and into the glory of God. I can imagine his smile as he embraced so many who have gone ahead, including Mom, just two and a half years ago, Dad nearly thirty-five years ago, and Granddad eighteen years ago. Dave and his wife Brenda cared for Granddad in his final years. Dave sure loved Granddad. We all did, but he and Granddad had something special. How blessed we've been to do life with such wonderful people whom we've loved so much, that missing them brings immense pain.

In the days we waited for Dave's earthly journey to end, and in the hours since he left us, I thought of our many times together. Dave was the fun one. He planned Granddad's eightieth birthday party complete with slides and script that had everyone laughing. He came up with the idea of surprising Mom and Dad on their twentieth anniversary. The party would take place at the ranch, but we had to get them out of the house so the guests could arrive. So, we blindfolded them, put them in the car, and Dave drove randomly through the valley to confuse them, so they didn't know we were taking them back home.

Dave had the idea to be Santa one year so the three of us climbed out of bed in the middle of the night, nightgowns rolled up under our coats (Colleen & I anyway) to do morning feeding chores while Dad & Mom slept. When our parents woke, a shepherd's cane, propped by the front of the door, included a note from Santa: "The chores are done. Merry Christmas." One afternoon, Mom put a ham in the oven for dinner. With tape recorder in hand, the three of us went to the farrowing barn where Dave squeezed a piglet until it squealed. Colleen and I recorded it and then at dinner, when Dad put the knife into the ham, Dave turned on the squealing piglet recording, the recorder hidden in his lap under the table. Dad stopped cutting the ham and off went the recording. Dad shook his head and reinserted the knife. On went the piglet recording again. Dad caught on, and we all howled with laughter.

Dave and I shared our birthday celebrations since they were two years minus one day apart. Mom always made two cakes so we wouldn't feel like we were really sharing! Of course, Grandma always brought a gift for little sister Colleen so she wouldn't feel left out. Yep, you got it, the youngest was spoiled!

Dave is the one I double-dated with in high school since my girlfriends were perfect dates for him and his friends were perfect dates for me. I guess Dad & Mom figured we'd help each other make good choices. Dave's also the one I fought with over who got to drive the car at college. Oh man, we had some doozies, but we always found our way back to friendship. As adults, Ron and I enjoyed pinochle games with him and Brenda, where the guys squared off against the gals! Since Dave can't correct me on this, I'm pretty sure we gals won most of the time!

It's impossible to relay all the memories. Perhaps one of my most heartfelt memories is when we were helping our mother in the final moments of her life. Surrounding her bed, our hands were joined together as Dave prayed over her. Then we all kissed her goodbye and Dave said, "I'll be right behind you Mom." None of us, including Dave, had any idea he too had cancer, cancer that would be discovered two weeks after Mom's passing.

As we prepare to celebrate my brother's life, I think his words are a great reminder; for aren't we all just right behind those who have passed from this life? We don't know when our earthly clock will chime its final hour, or when we will turn the page from this life to eternity; but we have today to make the memories, have long conversations, and plan the fun. One thing is certain though. When I cross over to heaven's glory, I'm pretty sure there will be an amazing celebration, because the FUN guy is there, using his God-given talent of planning events for something really special.

Dave, thanks for making our life journey better by giving of yourself, even if it meant having to knock a few rough spots off each other. We stuck it out, through thick and thin, honoring the people who made us family. You've now received your crown of life, and when God ordains it, we'll be right behind you.

"Blessed is the one who perseveres under trial because, having stood the test, that person will receive the crown of life that the Lord has promised to those who love him." James 1:12 (NIV).

Denise E. Johnson

Surrounded

We sent off brother Dave yesterday in the best of ways, surrounded by friends and family. Brenda and their girls did a beautiful job of planning his celebration of life, including a wonderful video tribute. Our nieces put together gorgeous flower arrangements. The sun was shining, making the chapel a bit warm as we squished into the small chapel with standing room only. It reminded me of the day Dave & Brenda got married; warm and crowded with Dave squished into his tux that arrived in a size much too small. That too had been a season of grief as Dad, confined at home in a hospital bed, lived out his final days.

    Yesterday was a special time being surrounded by my family. When the emotions are so deep, there is nothing quite as comforting as looking across the room and catching the reassuring smile of your adult child, or the hug from a grandchild, or the squeeze of your husband's hand.

    I was also touched by many others who came to support us: extended family, our sixth-grade teacher, long-time friends of our parents, friends from our childhood neighborhood, 4-H, college, and high school, some whom I hadn't seen in decades. In seasons like this, the past collides with the present, and time realigns as we again, share the same space with our common grief. Words were not needed. Just being hugged tightly while letting the tears flow is so healing. There is comfort in being surrounded by people.

    As I reflect on the day, I am filled with gratitude as well as a new perspective. I'm no longer the middle sibling: I'm the oldest surviving. In a few short years, God willing, my life span will carry on past Dave's. I feel a new sense of urgency to be with those who show their love by being there in body or spirit.

Life is getting shorter and our turn at glory is just ahead. In the days left, I want to hug the grieving, share the stories, and make the memories, for in the end, they are what carry forward those who remain. Until we meet again Dave, we will carry on, surrounding ourselves with the people who make life richer, just as you did for us.

"For to me, to live is Christ and to die is gain." Philippians 1:21 (NIV) There is joy in living a life that honors Christ, knowing upon our death, we gain eternity with our Lord and Savior.

Denise E. Johnson

Traction

Bam! I fell on my bottom so hard it jolted my whole body. It caught me completely by surprise. I felt a bit disorientated, so I remained sitting on the ground to gather myself. My elbow hit hard too. The sting of pain made me pause to evaluate, but I could still move it without pain. I'd probably have a pretty bruise though.

Ron and I had been hiking a very simple trail with our friend Roxi. It was a beautiful day. Just the right temperature with no breeze. We were seeing God's masterpiece of the desert outside of Mesa, Arizona. Being Montana natives, the cactuses and bushes were such a contrast from our majestic mountains and pine trees. What a sight to see. We'd made it about a mile up the trail without any problems but then, with the first slope heading back down, my foot slipped out from under me and left me sitting on my behind.

After I caught my breath, I stood, and we proceeded on. Even though I was a bit more cautious, moments later, my foot slipped again. This time I caught myself before crashing. What in the world was going on that I slipped so easily; twice now? I lifted my foot to examine the sole of the shoe. The problem became obvious. There was no tread left. These shoes were fine for street walking and biking, but on a trail, were like being on a frozen pond with ice skates.

My ineffective shoes caused me to think of other times when I'd fallen, perhaps not physically, but in other ways; like when I wasn't patient with my children because I hadn't taken time to rest, or made a decision without praying about it first, or plowed through my day without spending time with God, and then wondered why things didn't go so well.

Our daily walk with the Lord is as vital to life as a good pair of walking shoes on a desert trail. Without Him, we are ill-equipped on the trail of life. That can leave us ineffective. We can miss the moments He intends for us to help others or learn a lesson. We can grow stagnant and boring, not seeing opportunities for growth or change, or cause damage with missteps that are void of His wisdom and discernment. Although we can go through the motions of life, we may completely miss God's intention, wasting our lives on things that mean nothing.

John 15:5 says, "I am the vine; you are the branches. If you remain in me and I in you, you will bear much fruit; apart from me you can do nothing." (NIV). Yep, apart from him, we are as unprepared for our journey as if we had worn shoes without a tread on a hilly walking trail. Sitting on a trail with bone jarring pain isn't near as much fun as walking out the journey the Lord has waiting for us. When we stay connected to Him, He is our traction as we negotiate the decisions and circumstances of life. Happy trails my friends.

Denise E. Johnson

The Question

Days before Thanksgiving, I ran a quick errand to Target for supplies. As I surveyed the shelf, trying to determine which Greek yogurt to purchase for my recipe, a young family joined me in the yogurt aisle. When their little girl pointed excitedly to a particular product, the father with equal enthusiasm reached for one and asked, "This one?" The little girl shook her head no. The mother erupted and harshly corrected the father. "No, not that one! Dannon." She grabbed the Dannon yogurt from the shelf and then turned to the father and asked him, "Don't you even know her?"

I felt the sting of her words probably just as much as the father. I wanted to try to reverse the hurt I felt for the father as he snapped his hand back from the shelf. The beaming smile he'd had moments ago, as he tried to please his daughter, disappeared as he stepped away from the refrigerator case. I looked away, not wanting to add embarrassment to the moment, but as they left the aisle, I glanced back at them. His head hung in silent shame as he fell in behind the mother who pushed the cart.

Weeks later, I woke in the night and found myself tossing and turning, trying to go back to sleep, but instead, worrying. Complex family matters had robbed me of sleep as well as concerns with my volunteer ministry. I'd been writing legislative bills for months for the upcoming legislature and working on getting sponsors. The work group we'd been collaborating with started falling apart as politics and personal biases overshadowed actual goals. How were we going to hold it all together?

It was then, lying in the dark as sleep evaded me, that those words came to mind again. "Don't you even know Me?" It wasn't the harsh admonishment of the mother in Target, but rather a quiet loving nudge from my Father. As each worry entered my mind, like a steady wave gently touching my toes, I heard the question being repeated: "Don't you even know Me?" "Don't you even know Me?" "Don't you even know Me?"

I wrestled with my thoughts, clinging to the desire to hold onto them and then, like the tide gently rolling back to the sea, I let go of each worry because, yes, I knew Him. He was the God who took us, a childless couple and gave us five children and six grandchildren. He, after seasons of grief, brought incredible joy; saved a dying marriage and gave it new life; and brought all these years in child welfare reform to this season where we were poised for some true change.

He was the God who sent His son to be born in a manger and ultimately die, because there was no other way for His children to get to heaven.

I was reminded indeed; I did know Him. Knowing Him made all the difference in whether I was going to lie awake fretting, or put my worries to rest.

In busy seasons like Christmas, we often ask each other questions like: Do you have your shopping done? Who is coming for the holidays? Are you ready for Christmas? Perhaps the best question to ask is: Do you know Him? By knowing Him, our worries don't have to be so large, our pain so intense, and our outlook so bleak. He is the Savior of the world, and by knowing Him, we can rest in His care and purpose.

"So do not fear, for I am with you; do not be dismayed, for I am your God. I will strengthen you and help you; I will uphold you with my righteous right hand." Isaiah 41:10 (NIV).

Denise E. Johnson

Tender Mercies

As a young girl growing up on a ranch, I'd learned about the cycle of life. My first real taste of death came when I had to sell my 4-H steers. After months of raising them, cleaning out their stalls, teaching them to be led, and learning how to comb their hair for show, we were pals. Having to sell them left many a young 4-H'er huddled in a stall crying their eyes out, knowing their beloved animal was headed for slaughter. For me, I always went straight to the hayloft. Dad would come find me, wrap his arms around me, and just let me get it all out!

Then real losses happened. My best friend passed away when I was sixteen followed by another friend a month later. By the time I had reached thirty, I had also grieved the deaths of my grandmother, my father, and our first two children. As life went on, there were more goodbyes, including my remaining grandparents. When Mom passed away, it was a huge blow. Even with all my journeys through grief, I knew I'd need some help.

I learned the value of grief support when our infant children passed away. Back then, I joined a group called Rainbow. Being a part of a grief group isn't so much about sharing all our ragged emotions, but rather learning some coping skills while sharing the journey with others who are in the same season. I had healed well and met some wonderful friends in the process. So, with that as my experience, in this new season of grief, I decided to attend Grief Share.

As the weeks unfolded, one of the best takeaways was to look for God's tender mercies; little things that bring comfort. Perhaps it's a song that comes up on the radio or a call from a friend.

These tender mercies are ways God reminds us we are loved, and not forgotten in our pain. I began looking for God's tender mercies and discovered a letter Mom wrote where she spoke of how proud she was of me. I put it in my Bible where I can reference it whenever I'm missing her. I also found letters I had written home, filled with gratitude for my parents, including a letter I'd written to Mom shortly after our daughter Amy passed. Ironically, I found it on the anniversary of Amy's death. What salve that provided for my soul as I thought of that season, and how much Mom had helped me. God is so good to me!

In the few years since then, I've been intentional about looking for tender mercies God has given me to remember my mother. Then my brother Dave passed and another season of fresh grief brought new feelings. Just like grieving a mother is different than grieving a father or children, so is grieving a sibling. There is a strange sense of aloneness as you recognize there are fewer of you.

One day my sister Colleen called. She reminded me how her relatively new car often displays the wrong message on her console. Although she's tried to fix this, her car seems to have a mind of its own when it comes to displaying messages. After Mom passed, a text message notification came to Colleen from a friend, but instead of the friend's message, it was an old message from Mom. Colleen shared it with me then, and we both felt God's tender mercies as He gave us a reminder of Mom.

Well, it happened again. As Colleen drove across town, she got an alert of a text message, but instead of the actual message from her brother-in-law, her car verbalized a message from Dave. The message? "Finally beyond the pain. I'm relaxing now!" As she shared God's tender mercy, we both had a good cry.

Well, Colleen better not sell that car, ever! I love how God is using it to remind us how much he cares for us in our journey of grief with a tender message of His love.

Psalm 34:18 "The Lord is near to the brokenhearted and saves those who are crushed in spirit." (NIV).

Denise E. Johnson

My Vacation

I needed to make another trip to Helena to testify at an important legislative hearing, as well as assist in hosting a dinner event for a small group of legislators. The day started out a bit rough as I'd struggled to find the right outfit to wear. It caused me to be a bit behind schedule, putting frustration right at the beginning of the day.

Things quickly brightened when my daughter Kassi called. I could hear my three-year-old granddaughter Tilly in the background as she chimed in, "Hi Nanny," and then followed up with a short discourse of her daily activities. After a brief greeting, I reminded Kassi I was heading out of town. Hearing this, Tilly stated, "I don't want Nanny to go on vacation!" I couldn't help but laugh. This day was far from a vacation, but the only thing Tilly got out of the conversation was, I was leaving and she didn't want me to go.

The next day, Kassi called to say they would stop at the house around noon. Still making my way home, I told her I expected to arrive about noon as well. When my little crew arrived at my house ahead of me, Tilly was indignant. "It's time for Nanny to come home."

Her comments filled me with joy. Out of the mouths of babes; authentic raw truth, straight from the heart. I loved being with her as much as she expressed wanting to be with me.

Reflecting on her words, I wondered: Does the Lord ever feel like we went on vacation as our days swirl with activities? Does He long for us to come home and sit in His presence, attentive and available to commune with Him? Perhaps He even anticipates our literal coming home, our presence with Him in heaven at the end of this earthly life.

Someday, it will be time for us to go home, to be with Him for eternity. Until then, I want to have a heart like Tilly's; one that is raw, authentic, and aching for closeness to the Lord, with a hunger for His presence in the moments of my day. What about you? Maybe it's time for you to come home too!

1 Kings 8:61 "And you, your lives must be totally obedient to God, our personal God, following the life path he has cleared, alert and attentive to everything he has made plain this day." (MSG).

Denise E. Johnson

Running Out of Air

Ron and I took a drive to Red Lodge, a small community an hour away. We ate lunch and meandered around the quaint streets before starting back home. When we crossed the final set of railroad tracks and headed north toward home, the low tire warning came on the dash. I selected the tire pressure indicator and noted the front passenger tire only had seventeen pounds of pressure. We must have picked up a nail. Since I'd just left the road closest to the tire shop, I took the next road to circle back.

    For the next five miles, I tried to drive slow enough to be safe, but fast enough to not completely run out of air. As I did, the tire pressure continued to drop…fifteen, thirteen, eleven, nine, seven. With each mile slowly passing, I prayed aloud. "Lord, please get us there before we run out of air." When we finally pulled into the tire shop parking lot, I let out a heavy sigh! Miraculously, three pounds of air pressure remained, just enough to get us to the shop.

    My low tire experience reminded me of my own life. I was running out of air too. For the past three months, I'd driven back and forth to Helena to testify at the legislature and defend bills. It had been tough, really tough. We'd lost some important bills, key relationships were strained due to lack of communication, and politics and personalities had overshadowed good policy. With only a month left in session, little time remained to right some wrongs.

    Overshadowing the time constraints was a very real awareness of the enemy's attack. Every member of our team of advocates was experiencing personal traumas; not just simple things, but large life-changing crises. Then came horrifying news that a fellow advocate had been murdered by her estranged husband, shouting about the importance of our work. Today's zoom call only heightened our urgency when we learned a child had been hospitalized because of an abusive parent's lack of care.

As we navigated these various challenges, we were all working hard to get an important bill passed; one to protect children from domestic violence. Surprisingly, opposition came from the very organization that should have supported this effort. Politics and money have a way of corrupting and opening the door for the enemy's attack.

Our team was numb and exhausted. We knew we'd done everything humanly possible to educate and raise awareness for the desperate need for this legislation. We needed a clear path forward and yet; every effort was met with more roadblocks. We'd taken this as far as we could go. Now we needed a miracle.

2 Chronicles 20:15, 17 came to mind: "*Do not be afraid or discouraged because of this vast army. For the battle is not yours, but God's. Take up your positions; stand firm and see the deliverance the Lord will give you. Do not be afraid; do not be discouraged. Go out to face them tomorrow, and the Lord will be with you." (NIV).*

The words filtered through my mind, realizing that although we were in a battle, it was the Lord's. Would the battle be over tomorrow, or even the next day? I don't know, but I was certain of one thing: I'd been called to stand firm, to wait with expectation for His deliverance, and to not become discouraged or afraid. The Lord was with us. He would deliver us in His time and season!

Denise E. Johnson

My Own Personal Snowstorm

I woke up with a crazy mixture of excitement, fatigue, anxiousness, and a sense of urgency. I'd been invited to a leadership conference in sunny Fort Worth, Texas, and couldn't wait to enjoy 70-degree weather. That sure sounded nice compared to -1 degree with the nasty Montana winter storm. After my flight today, I planned to meet a new friend for dinner. It would be a fun getaway.

Although I couldn't wait to get there, things were moving at warp speed at the Legislature. If the child welfare reform bills we'd been working on didn't get through in the next week, they would be DEAD! There were still over twenty bills that needed to go through the process. The trip couldn't have come at a worse time.

I got ready for the day and then packed with haste. I needed to be on a zoom call for a hearing at 9:00 am. The muscles in my neck and back were tight with tension. Based on how the bills were heard, it was possible I'd need to leave for the airport before I had a chance to testify. Perhaps I could keep the zoom link going on my drive to the airport! That still left two testimonies I needed to write since they had just been scheduled for hearings on Friday, which I definitely couldn't attend.

My fingers flew across the keyboard, trying to maximize the few hours before I needed to leave. A message popped up in my email: "Your flight is on schedule." I tried to work faster. Then eight minutes later, "Your flight has been canceled". Both disappointment and relief swept through me. I realized that even though I was anxious to get there, I needed this one more day to address the urgent issues at hand.

As the day unfolded, I testified on the bills, wrote a proposed amendment for a bill, and wrote the additional testimonies for the Friday hearings. Two of my children also stopped and we enjoyed some time catching up. I even got in a much-needed hour of downtime to play Canasta with my husband.

The next morning, a family matter arose that absolutely needed to be attended to. In fact, if it didn't get addressed, I wouldn't be getting on the plane. Within a few hours, things were back on track and Ron dropped me off at the airport. Going through security I thought, "Thank God my flight got canceled so I was home where I needed to be these past twenty-four hours."

A grounded airplane due to a snowstorm felt like a gift. In fact, it almost seemed like God had done that just for me! If so, I'm sorry to my fellow travelers, but I am so grateful. God knew I needed an extra day to be present for matters I couldn't have planned nor anticipated, allowing my day to serve His purposes and my sanity!

James 4:13-15 "Now listen, you who say, 'Today or tomorrow we will go to this or that city, spend a year there, carry on business and make money. Why, you do not even know what will happen tomorrow. What is your life? You are a mist that appears for a little while and then vanishes. Instead, you ought to say, 'If it is the Lord's will, we will live and do this or that." (NIV) I'm good with that!

Denise E. Johnson

Rebuilding

The tall wooden tower Papa and four-year-old Leila had been constructing suddenly came crashing down. Their masterpiece, now a pile of stick rubble. Leila's eyes flew open in surprise, her expression filled with uncertainty as she watched for her Papa's reaction. Was this a disaster or part of the fun? He laughed and convinced her they could rebuild it. Her concern turned to a smile as she and Papa began stacking the sticks again.

Something about this moment, watching the tower be built, seeing it fall, observing Leila's response to the crash, but most especially, her pause as she waited for Papa's reaction. It caused me to think of "towers" in life that sometimes, even after much planning and time, come crashing down. Marriages that end, relationships that go south, businesses that fail, and the endless list of investments of time and energy that don't turn out as planned.

Life is full of tower crashing moments. They are often accompanied with feelings of disappointment, frustration, grief, anger, and other emotions that are important to process. Like Leila, we too can focus on the pile of rubble or look to our Papa. You know what our good Father has to say about it?

"I'm about to rebuild you with stones of turquoise, lay your foundations with sapphires, construct your towers with rubies, your gates with jewels and your walls with precious stones. You'll be built solid, grounded in righteousness, far from any trouble---nothing to fear. This is what God's servants can expect. I'll see to it that everything works out for the best." Isaiah 54:11 – 17 (MSG).

We all have disasters and failed attempts. That's part of living, but when it comes time to rebuild, we often have a better perspective. We realize there are weaknesses that need to be reinforced, areas that need more thought, energy that needs to be invested where perhaps we didn't the first time around. Our rebuilding gives us the opportunity to improve on what we already know. It will be better than what we built the first time. When we trust God to the outcomes, we can be assured that out of the rubble will rise solid, grounded results, filled with God's best for us. He is a good and loving God.

Denise E. Johnson

Random Reminders

I had just planted myself in the Returns line at Hobby Lobby, wanting to return a picture that was a bit wonky. I loved the saying on the picture, but when I went to hang it on the wall, I realized it was warped and thus wouldn't lay flat on the wall. Standing there holding the warped picture, I was deep in thought about my own life, which also felt a bit warped. We were in a season of great pain and turmoil, as tragedies were playing out due to unwise decisions made by one of our loved ones. As a result, our entire family felt trauma to some level. We hoped in time, there would be healing.

With my thoughts on our crisis, I realized the beautiful young lady ahead of me was talking to me. I hadn't even heard her, but she repeated her question, asking if I thought the silver Sharpie would show up on the black surface she was holding. I remembered our daughter's wedding and how we had used a gold Sharpie on a black background. It hadn't shown up as we'd hoped, so I assured the young lady ahead of me that the silver was a great choice.

My eyes shifted to the cross she was holding so I complimented her on it.

"It's a gift for a wedding today." Then she went on to explain she had noticed this one yesterday, but then purchased another. However, during the night, she realized she preferred the first choice so came back to exchange her purchase for this cross. Oh, a girl after my own heart. I'm notorious for overthinking my decisions, especially in the middle of the night.

In the moments that followed, she shared the most tender story of a groom who was going to be married without his best friend in attendance, his sister. She then told me the sister had tragically passed away, but during her life, had given crosses to her brother. This gift would be the newlyweds first cross to hang on their wall; a gift from both the sister who no longer was with them, and this young lady who understood the significance.

By now I choked back tears, so touched by her story. As the cashier motioned her forward, the young lady turned to me and said, "You know, God always uses our tragedies and our tears. He never wastes them."

I nodded in agreement, unable to choke out words. It was a truth I knew very well, but standing behind her with my warped picture reflecting on my warped life circumstances, there couldn't have been a better time to be reminded.

I almost stepped out of line with my wonky picture and brought it back home. Maybe I needed a reminder of the special message delivered to me that day, but I returned it. I knew the chance encounter with this young woman had been carefully arranged by my loving Father. Yes, even this season of hardship and tragedy would be used by Him. I just needed to keep my eyes on Him and trust Him to the outcomes.

Romans 8:28 "And we know that for those who love God all things work together for good, for those who are called according to His purposes." (ESV).

Denise E. Johnson

Broken

Crash! The sound gave me a sick feeling in my stomach. There on the floor, in hundreds of pieces, was the beautiful red glass. It belonged to a set of drinking glasses, an antique family heirloom. That wasn't the worst of it! What could be worse? Well, it wasn't even mine.

I'd been having lunch at my dear friend Pam's home, along with friends from Bible study. As we were clearing up the dishes, without realizing the glass was there, my arm swept over the counter and then, CRASH! I apologized profusely, knowing its significance, but in her usual grace, Pam told me not to worry about it. Although she'd dismissed the entire issue, I couldn't. Upon returning home, I put my husband to work looking for a matching glass on the internet. We scoured multiple sites and when we found a set of four glasses that looked like they might match, we ordered them.

In the days that followed, waiting for the replacement glasses to arrive, I couldn't get the CRASH out of my mind. It made me think back to the days teaching my children to ride a bike. We'd start out on the grass with me running next to them, helping them steer and remain upright. If they tipped over, the soft grass buffered the fall. I'd prop them back up and encourage them to give it another try.

Reflecting on those earlier years, I realized it was a picture of God. He's a good Father who wants to be beside us as we learn to navigate through life's challenges. He wants to teach us how to keep our lives in balance and help us succeed. If we try to do life without Him, it's no different than putting a toddler on a bike without any assistance. It will result in a CRASH, but no matter how badly we've CRASHED or wandered away from the Lord, He is just a word away. All we need to do is ask Him to help us. He is the great repairer of the broken.

However, sometimes the lesson is in the broken, as in the case of the red glass. Days later, when the glasses I ordered were delivered to my doorstep, I couldn't wait to see how closely they matched. Back at Pam's, we lined up one of the remaining glasses with the ones we ordered. They weren't exactly the same, but pretty close. Pam was thrilled. Her glasses have another story now, and I suspect in the future, when she serves water in them, she will think of the broken glass as well as the replacements that are not quite the same.

When we allow God to heal our brokenness, we won't be the same as before either. We will have a new story; a testimony of what God has done. For once we've experienced His rescue and repair, we won't view life the same. So, here's the question: Why, why, why would anyone want to live life without God? He is right here, wanting to help guide us. He is a good, good Father who desires the best of life for each of us. He can handle life's CRASHES because it is His desire for us to prosper. Even better, He can help us avoid the CRASH altogether if we allow Him to help us navigate the complexities of life.

Psalm 145:7-9: "They shall abundantly utter the memory of thy great goodness; and shall sing of thy righteousness. The Lord is gracious, and full of compassion; slow to anger, and of great mercy. The Lord is good to all; and his tender mercies are over all his works" (KJV).

Nahum 1:7: "The LORD is good, a refuge in times of trouble. He cares for those who trust in him." (NIV).

Jeremiah 29:11: "For I know the plans I have for you,' declares the Lord, 'plans to prosper you and not to harm you, plans to give you hope and a future." (NIV).

Denise E. Johnson

She Chose Life

Shock was all I could muster when I learned my beautiful, talented, smart, eighteen-year-old daughter was pregnant. She had plans for college, plans to be a surgeon. She had a six-week mission trip scheduled for Africa, including time with a medical mission team. She graduated from high school a semester early to accomplish all this. That all changed with news of her pregnancy. **But she chose life.**

Society allows for other options which might have seemed easier. She could have avoided telling us. She could have continued with her plans, and spared herself the shame and judgment others pile on when they discovered she was pregnant. Besides, who would have known? She wouldn't have to be accountable to anyone, right? **But she chose life**.

It meant she chose her baby's life over all her plans. It meant taking a job so she could provide for her son rather than going to college. It meant choosing to face the opinions of others while standing firm in her convictions, and facing her fear of being an unwed mom. **She chose life.**

As her parents, it meant watching as her friends went off to college. It meant grieving for her childhood that was now over. It meant realizing her life could become very, very hard. At times it meant walking that fine line between empowering versus enabling (which we probably didn't get right all the time) because we still wanted our amazing daughter and her child to have a wonderful life. **She chose life.**

It meant giving up time to work or play, because we were helping her with him. It meant having hard conversations about priorities, relationships, and life, because it was even more important now that she had a son. It meant helping with night shifts and rocking a teething child, because we knew there is nothing easy about being a mama. **She chose life.**

It meant God gave us a new baby to love in our later years. It meant rearranging our house to accommodate a toddler who could dismantle everything within seconds. It meant toys strewn about, fingerprints on the mirrors, creating new schedules, working around naps and feeding times, and taking on babysitting duties. It wasn't always convenient and it wasn't always easy.

Because she chose life, we have a beautiful grandson who is the light of our lives. God brought this child into the world for kingdom work, with a special purpose and plan. By some miracle, He destined this precious little boy to be a part of our lives. The trajectory of our lives and hers forever changed. Back then the trajectory looked harder, but now, looking back, it was exactly as it was meant to be.

Our amazing daughter has now added three beautiful daughters and a handsome kind husband, Lucas, to our family. She is pursuing her medical career and using her talents and experiences to guide other young women in her church ministry. Her life has produced joy, fulfillment, and commitment that is admirable. I am so proud of how well my daughter navigated this challenging season of her life, and used it to grow in ways that honored God and the lives of her children and family.

All because she chose life.

Denise E. Johnson

For Heaven's Sake

I have been praying for a special young lady with fervor. I love her dearly and since she's been going through some hard things, I was concerned for her, especially since her once chatty personality had become sullen and withdrawn. In an effort to create better communication between us, I'd purchased a deck of conversation cards, specifically geared toward her age. Anytime we were together, we'd pull out cards and ask each other random questions. It proved to be fun and generated some interesting conversation.

Last week she pulled out a card with this question: "What do you think will happen after you die?" My response brought a brief testimony about my decision to ask Jesus to be my Savior and thus, knowing I would go to heaven. Her response alluded to reincarnation. I tried to initiate some discussion on truth vs. fiction, but she challenged me, "How do you know heaven is real since you haven't been there?" I briefly answered, but didn't want things to get tense, so I let it go and we picked another question.

The next time I saw her, I wanted to circle back. "You asked how I knew heaven was real." Then I shared Colton Burpo's story based on his book, "Heaven is for Real." I also shared how my own father told us of his heavenly experience in the days before he died. Her body language showed what she soon verbalized, "I'm not interested in this subject." I gently pressed. "Honey, you might not be interested, but it's very important. I want you to be in heaven with me." She responded, "I don't want to learn any more about this right now." I let it drop, hoping seeds had been planted.

Since I'd promised ice cream, we headed to Dairy Queen. We were greeted by an older man who was contagiously happy.

When he turned to serve another customer, she commented on the nice man. As he returned to complete our order, he stated, "I'm happy because I just checked out of hospice." I gave him an inquisitive look, and he responded. "I had sepsis and was told I would die. I did die, and I went to heaven, but God told me it wasn't my time, and I had to go back."

Goosebumps trickled down my arms as he continued, "When you've been to heaven, you see life differently."

"I can only imagine," I responded and then added, "You really ought to write your story."

His head was already nodding, "Yes, I have the medical records that confirm I was dead. I plan to write about it."

We visited a bit longer and then our order was ready. Since it was closing time, we took the ice cream to the car. As we wandered to the car, I couldn't hold back. "Well, what did you think of that?"

A little smile tugged at her lips as she responded. "With that coming up just after we were talking, that's quite a coincidence. I guess God wants me to learn something I didn't think I wanted to."

I couldn't hold back my chuckle. "Yes, God is good that way." With the topic now reopened, I added, "This subject of heaven is particularly fresh for me. My mom went to heaven four years ago tomorrow. I miss her and am so glad I'll get to see her again. I want you to be there too."

We talked a little longer and then it was time for our next stop. I trust there will be another opportunity. One thing is certain, she no longer has to take my word for it. She has now personally met someone who went to heaven and came back to tell others about it! *John 14:2-3: "My Father's house has many rooms; if that were not so, would I have told you that I am going there to prepare a place for you? And if I go and prepare a place for you, I will come back and take you to be with me so that you also may be where I am." (NIV).*

Denise E. Johnson

Just Ask

As Thanksgiving neared, I knew my son Josh wanted to invite his girlfriend to join us. Recently, there had been a misunderstanding that caused some hurt feelings. As far as I was concerned, it was water under the bridge. She was more than welcome to join us, but I waited to make the invitation because I wanted my son to ask. Learning to ask for his wants and needs was an important part of communicating and development as a man of character. So, I held out, waiting.

    About four days ahead of the holiday, he and I were discussing the menu and rather tentatively, he finally asked. "Of course she's welcome," I answered. An unseen tension in the room seemed to pop like a balloon when touched by a pin. Our conversation relaxed and felt comfortable like usual.

    I thought of other times when asking matters. I appreciate when the grandchildren ask for a treat rather than just taking one. I appreciate when my children ask if I would help them, rather than just assuming I would. My 'yes' answer was the same regardless, but it was nice to be asked. It showed respect and authority for me as their mother/grandmother. It wasn't like I was on some power trip, but asking makes me feel honored and appreciated. Good manners are developed in the process.

    Reflecting on this caused me to think of Father God. He's a much better Father than I am as a human mother and yet, He also wants us to ask for our needs and wants. He knows my requests before they even leave my tongue, but by asking, it shows humility, respect, and proper alignment of who I am as His child. Asking shows reverence to His authority and creates communication between us, just like it did with my son.

Asking also brings gratitude. When a request is granted, a thank you is appropriate. As the treats come out of the pantry, there is a thank you. As we babysit so the adults can have an evening out, there is a thank you. A big happy circle of communication leaves us feeling needed and appreciated. It creates warm feelings as we recognize the value of each other in our lives, in the small and large details. Just like it pleased me to say yes to my son's request, our Father is pleased when our requests align with His will, and He can say 'yes". It develops our character and creates a dependence on our heavenly Father.

God is a good and loving Father. It's His desire to bless us. He wants us to ask. It pleases Him when we do, even if it feels trite and small. His answer can't be 'yes' to a request that is never asked. When His answer is 'yes', may our praise and gratitude reach the ears of our Father. For all glory and honor is His!

John 16:24: "Until now you have asked nothing in my name. Ask and you will receive, that your joy may be full." (ESV).

Denise E. Johnson

Oops!

Please tell me you've done this too. While busy paying bills, I received an exciting text message from my friend Lisa. I quickly texted her back: "You amaze me. That is awesome. You have a very bright future."

She wrote back, "I amaze you?"

"You do."

"You made me cry. I feel like such a failure."

I paused and looked closer at my phone. Failure? What? Then I realized my encouraging messages had gone to another friend who texted me right after Lisa. Therefore, she had gotten Lisa's messages.

I felt sadness as her words soaked in. A failure? This friend was amazing too and had I been intentional about sending her a text, I could have easily sent the exact message to her. She was someone I admired as well. Today, clearly, she needed an encouraging word too.

Since I didn't want her to know about my texting error, I ended it with, "Keep your chin up. Decide what you're going to do that will amaze you!"

The accidental text reminded me to be more focused on being an encourager, and to look for opportunities to build others up. This life can be discouraging and a simple text to remind others of their value is an easy thing to do.

God is pretty amazing too, don't you think? He took a busy moment when I wasn't as focused as I should have been, and used it to bless someone else. Only God could have known how much she needed to hear those encouraging words.

1 Thessalonians 5:11 reminds us: "Therefore encourage one another and build one another up, just as you are doing." (ESV).

Ephesians 4:29: "Let no corrupting talk come out of your mouths, but only such as is good for building up, as fits the occasion, that it may give grace to those who hear." (ESV).

Romans 15:2: "Let each of us please his neighbor for his good, to build him up." (ESV).

Denise E. Johnson

Simple Treasurers

To say Mom was a great saver would be an understatement. She saved anything and everything. Today while going through some of her saved items, I came across a letter I'd written to my grandparents years ago. I took a moment to read it: Dad had twelve litters of piglets to attend to, my sister was waiting for her ewes to lamb, school was good, and my social calendar was full. We planned to go to Darrell and Lana's house for the Super Bowl. Darrell worked for my dad, and Lana, nine years my senior, was like the big sister I never had, always ready with advice on boys or life. We often got together to play board games and even took a family vacation together, eight of us piled in a Winnebago. What fun!

As I finished reading the letter, I tucked it back into the envelope and noticed another yellowed envelope. It didn't appear to have anything in it, so I turned it over. Scrawled across the back, written in my dad's handwriting: "Denise, call Pam". That did it; the sentiment of the first letter along with this note caused tears to rush to my eyes, as memories filled my mind.

I thought of Dad's office where the house phone sat on his desk. In the swirl of paperwork, he likely wrote on the first available slip of paper. Seeing his handwriting caused a lump in my throat. I hadn't seen it in quite some time, since he'd passed away thirty-five years ago.

My mind then went to Pam. She had been my closest friend in high school. We were inseparable, and although we went to different high schools, we both participated in several extra-curricular clubs, and had plans to room together at 4-H camp that summer. Her family was a second family to me. Then unexpectedly,

Pam died. One night we had been talking on the phone about our boyfriends and social world, and the next morning she was gone.

Weeks later, Lana was hospitalized with hepatitis. I remember visiting her there, holding her hand and looking into her jaundiced face and eyes. She expressed sorrow about Pam's death. Then Lana died too, leaving behind her three young children. She was only twenty-five.

That summer, responsibilities mixed with grief kept our family going as we spent time with Pam's family, and tried to cope while caring for Lana's three children so their father could work. Then somehow, forty-five years later, I held scraps of paper that testified of the fullness of Lana and Pam in my life so many years ago.

A simple letter and a quickly scribbled message; treasures that surely mean more to me now than when they were written so long ago. Mom must have recognized their value too. Good save Mom.

Finding these made me ponder: What was I leaving for my loved ones to remind them of our life together? In our fast-paced, text and delete, move-on world, what might they stumble upon that would cause them to reflect on days we shared? I thought of the photo books and my journals filled with lessons learned. Perhaps my blogs. Regardless, I want to be more intentional about what I'm leaving behind, so my true treasure, my family, will have the joy of stirring up memories too.

Matthew 6:19 - 21 "Do not store up for yourselves treasures on earth, where moths and vermin destroy, and where thieves break in and steal. But store up for yourselves treasures in heaven, where moths and vermin do not destroy, and where thieves do not break in and steal. For where your treasure is, there your heart will be also. (NIV).

Denise E. Johnson

The Tapestry

I've heard it said, our lives are a bit like a tapestry. As we look at it from the bottom side, we see a mess of threads, meandering haphazardly without much design. Once we get to see the topside, from God's perspective, we will see a beautiful piece of art. As someone who once enjoyed needlework and cross-stitch, it's something I can relate to. Many times, I hid an unwanted knot or fixed a missed stitch on the backside. I knew it wouldn't show on topside once the backside was finished off.

As I wrap up this book, filled with some of the Awe God moments in life, it's a bit like getting a peek at the top of the tapestry. I can see how some of those messy threads created something marvelous for God's glory. I began to understand why I needed to experience certain situations and people, because it prepared and trained me for something ahead.

For example, had we not experienced our failed adoption, I might not have understood the pain of being forced to relinquish my child. Later when God called me to advocate for children and families who are involved with child protective services, I understood their pain. I knew how it felt to be consumed, not knowing where my child was, or even if they were okay.

Had I not gone toe-to-toe with my supervisor about her poor decision to allow a pedophile into the preschool, I might not have understood the voids in the law when it comes to protecting vulnerable children. That experience prepared me for a season in life when I wrote bills, worked with legislators, and testified at hearings to create better laws for children. All of it was outside of my comfort zone, but all was allowed by God to give me experiences and courage for what He had purposed in my life; helping me to take a stand for children and give them a voice.

As I recognized these connections, I wondered: How many other times has God been in the details, orchestrating behind the scenes when I wasn't aware? How often has He intervened or protected me without my knowledge, or allowed a teaching lesson so I was better prepared down the road? Likely many, many more times than I could ever fathom.

In the days ahead, I'm sure He will reveal many more Awe God moments, so I'll continue documenting them. Perhaps there will be an Awe God 2.0 in the future. While we're on the subject, perhaps you've experienced Awe God moments as well, ones your loved ones would enjoy reading about. Be brave. Start writing them down.

Psalm 32:8 tells us: "I will instruct you and teach you in the way you should go; I will counsel you with my eye upon you," (NIV).

If we will allow, God will counsel and teach us so we're prepared for kingdom work, creating a tapestry that gives glory to Him. Until God calls me home, I consider it a privilege to be on the bottom side of the tapestry, poking the needle through to the top as He guides it. What a joy it will be to see the final tapestry of my life, created under the watchful eye of our heavenly Father.

To God be the glory,
Denise

Denise E. Johnson

Other Books written by Denise E. Johnson

Love To Give

Denise shares their personal journey to become parents. Their story is one of tragedy and hope as they found a way to move on through their faith. An inspirational true-life story of grief, healing, hope and God's amazing plan that will inspire you to see the gift of children from a new perspective.

For The Children

This novel presents a rare look inside foster care through the eyes of children, families, and professionals who work on behalf of children in crisis. A powerful story that shines a light on sensitive issues so often misunderstood and left unspoken in the complex child welfare system.

www.ingramcontent.com/pod-product-compliance
Lightning Source LLC
Chambersburg PA
CBHW030435010526
44118CB00011B/643